A Life Divined

The insight and inspiration of

HAMISH MILLER

Compiled and considered by

Nigel Twinn

from extensive discussions with Hamish during
the last months of his life 2009 - 2010

First published in 2010 by:

Penwith Press
PO Box 11
Hayle, Cornwall
TR27 6YF

ISBN 978-0-9533316-2-8

Printed by TJ International Ltd.
Trecenus Industrial Estate
Padstow, Cornwall
PL28 8RW

FSC

The paper used for the text pages of this book is FSC certified. FSC
(The Forest Stewardship Council) is an international network to promote
responsible management of the world's forests.

Contents

Acknowledgements

I am indebted to many people for helping me to make this book a reality.

Amongst those who have contributed in their various ways are:

Alan Neal
Annie Turner
Ba Miller
Billy Gawn
Frances Lewis
Helen Lamb
Huw Lloyd-Jones
Jim Lyons
John Olivey
Martin Shoesmith
Michael Sherwin
Palden Jenkins
Paul Broadhurst
Peter Bousfield
Ros Twinn
Rose Wood
Sheila Nevins
Sig Lonegren
Tim Walter

The late Colin Bloy and John Michell
- and the even later Daniel Bernoulli

but most of all to Hamish Miller, who had more faith
in my ability to make it happen than I had myself.

List of Illustrations

Many of the photographs used in this book were found in Hamish's files after his death and their precise date and origin is unknown. If, however, the original photographer is determined at a later date, an appropriate accreditation will be given in any reprint of this book.

Preface

On a wet afternoon in the late 1980's I made a remarkable connection with people from another dimension.

I don't watch daytime television, or at least I wouldn't admit to it, yet here on my screen was a low-tech cameo video featuring two men driving across southern England, with the driver waving a couple of metal rods about in a quite startling manner. For a few moments, I thought I had entered the realm of someone in a cult sci-fi production - you know, where the hero gets a personal message from aliens through his domestic TV.

These chaps, however, despite clearly thoroughly enjoying the whole process, were very real and deadly serious. They were claiming to have found earth energy lines (whatever that meant) running from the far south west, through areas of counties that were intimately familiar to me, and off into the North Sea via the coast of East Anglia. I was caught between fascination and disbelief - but I was hooked. It was as if someone had just flicked a button and my monochrome world had gone into technicolour.

To compound the mystery, the programme seemed to finish before it had begun and in those pre-historic times before the internet, there was no obvious way to find out any more about the strange duo, whether they were scientists or scoundrels - or even if the whole thing was a spoof. Yet I was left feeling that I had chanced on a mysterious new world, somehow nested inside the time and space of the one that I could see around me. No-one else had seen the film and no-one could understand why I thought it was so interesting. In a strange, perhaps intuitive way, I knew I had glimpsed an alternative future.

I later discovered that the navigator was the author, Paul Broadhurst, and the genial wild-man driver with the bits of bent wire was the dowser, Hamish Miller - and that they really had slipped into a parallel way of sensing the world.

Over the subsequent decades I took up the lost art of divining myself in a modest manner and, to my great delight, met Hamish on the same plane of existence and occasionally corresponded with him.

On the strength of reading a few brief articles that I had written for Dowsing Today, the sensitive Scot suggested that I write a book - indeed he ended each of our infrequent conversations with the same refrain 'You should write a book'. My response was equally repetitive. How could I write a book without any proper material?

This little game of harmless verbal ping-pong carried on for several years. Then, in the spring of 2009, as part of a response to an email on an unrelated subject, Hamish happened to mention that he had been diagnosed with a heart problem and, having already had more brushes with the world beyond the veil than most of us put together, he was 'rather excited' about what might follow. A penny dropped and I suddenly realised that the book I could write was almost literally staring me in the face - a book about Hamish himself. Having indicated that he thought he was moving into the twilight of this particular cycle and being quite comfortable with his lot, time suddenly seemed to be of the essence.

After a couple of glasses of wine one Sunday evening, I mentioned, as casually as you can under such circumstances, to my wife Ros, that I thought I might bounce the idea of working on a biography of Hamish off the potential victim. Expecting a non-committal response, I was a bit taken back when she responded, clearly and unemotionally 'Yes that's what you should be doing. You should be writing a book about Hamish.' Emboldened by the output of this one-woman focus group, I sent off a tentative email to the legendary dowser.

Whether on not you believe in synchronicity, or even in co-incidence, some things do seem destined to happen. This book is one of them. I was astonished with his response.

He told me that he had been thinking of updating his autobiographical work *It's Not Too Late*, but had been unsure quite how to set about it - and anyway, if the safety curtains really were starting to move across, was this really the time to spend months, if not years, trying to sum up the past and give it a bit of added perspective, when the onrushing future demanded his full attention.

Then I think The Management (we will hear more of them later - NT), as they tend to do, made a quiet suggestion that perhaps someone else's interpretation of the whole thing might be more effective and get to a wider public. I immediately rejected the thought on the grounds that it was a colossal arrogance to think that anyone else might be interested enough in what I've been doing to spend real time on such an ethereal project. But the niggling thought wouldn't go away. During these times of "half-awake" it kept coming back. Who on earth could I possibly approach to do it, who would not misunderstand the reasons for wanting it to happen? The answer came in loud, clear and unequivocally - "Nigel Twinn".

Suddenly it all fell into place and I came within an ace of telephoning, but I couldn't think how to approach the subject on the telephone. A letter? . . . An email? . . . Solution - Nigel apparently gets a message directly from The Management and says "let's stop pussyfooting around and make it happen"!!

Bizarrely, this is a book that started and finished as an Obituary. One day, I was reading an account of a chap who had lived to a good age, but whose only real achievement, according to the writer, seemed to be that he quite liked gardening. This seemed a rather poor show for a lifetime of personal endeavour and, perhaps a bit pompously, I felt I could have written something considerably better. My train of thought strayed on to people whose obituaries I could conceivably write - and it occurred to me that for someone like my occasional correspondent Hamish Miller, I might be able to compile a few quite interesting paragraphs. It further occurred to me that as he was still very much with us, he could participate in the process and he would then get the obituary he would have wanted. It was a daft idea, and I cast it out my mind. Only after we had got underway with this book, and I got to know him better, did I confide my musings about a living obituary to him. Unpredictable as ever, and far from being affronted, he thought it was outrageously funny - and in his last email to me in January 2010 he reminded me to 'get the bit about the obituary into the book somewhere'. So, if you're watching, Hamish, here it is!

When we started this project, Hamish had been diagnosed with a serious heart problem and had been given between three months and three years to live. If he had wrapped himself in cotton wool, he might have lived a little longer than he did, but that was never going to be his way. Life was to be lived - and lived to the full. In the end we had about seven months working on the material - and I was very grateful for that. We recorded all of our conversations on Digital Voice Recorder and Hamish had two chances to read through an advanced draft. So, I was pleased, in the end, just to be left with the topping and tailing of the book.

For the first 50-odd years of his life, Hamish appears to have been a fairly ordinary bloke - more intelligent than many, more ambitious than some and certainly more successful than most - but for all that, not someone you would pick out from the crowd in the pub as the herald of a new dawn.

Then, in 1982, he suffered a serious illness, effectively died on the operating table and returned to tell the tale. Near Death Experiences (NDE) are rare, but not that rare. Invariably, such a traumatic experience changes the outlook of the participant, often dramatically for the better.

Hamish left behind his career as a successful businessman and joined what he then perceived to be the real world.

How you see and how you sense the world around you is, in great measure, derived from your own history and your own heritage. It's coloured by your own personal baggage - some of which, arguably, comes with you from somewhere even deeper in the past.

Most of us go through a slow personal evolution, punctuated by the odd tiny eureka moment, which just might appear on daytime TV. But for those who have been through an NDE, there is a sudden fault in the timeline. Nothing can ever seem quite the same again. Old needs and desires, and established ways of looking at the world, no longer seem so solid, nor even so valid. Insight, or enlightenment as some schools refer to it, can come in many forms and can have many implications. For Hamish, the NDE left him with a New World View and he never looked back.

As the story unfolded, Hamish discovered the ancient and arcane art of dowsing and the rest, as they say, is history - albeit a thoroughly riveting tranche of it.

If you have never heard of dowsing, let alone Hamish Miller, don't be put off. This is not a book about dowsing as such. There are plenty of good guides on how to get started on dowsing and I list some of them later in this book. No, this is in part a book about one man's experience of what light is thrown on the here and now by the practice of dowsing - and on where the art can lead the enthusiastic pilgrim.

Dowsing is just a tool - a very special kind of tool. Just as travelling can show you other parts of the country that you have seen on the news, or other parts of the world you have heard about; just as reading can give you an insight into the ideas and perspectives of other people, so dowsing can show you a cosmos you had never even considered. It's a multi-dimensional matrix - and it's in your own front room.

Most of us go through periods of feeling that 'there must be something more to life than this'. Dowsing shows that there really is more - and that it is both 'within you and without you', as the Beatles once said.

You don't need drugs or alcohol; you don't need to spend years in some esoteric retreat in the mountains (at least, not to get started) and, even better, you don't have to be academically talented or well educated. Being stoned, rich, ostentatiously clever or wonderfully well-read actually gets in the way. What you do need is an open mind, an open heart and a willingness to expand your horizons.

My one word of caution is that, like a cow chewing contentedly in a field, once you have looked over the wall and seen what is out there, chewing the same old grass never seems quite so satisfying again. You can't realistically go into denial when you know that everything about you is humming and vibrating with the energy of life. Once the rods have moved for you, you would have to be some sort of fossil not to appreciate that there is a boundless universe waiting to be explored - and that's just the beginning.

Like Hamish, you will discover that it's all 'rather exciting'.

Part One

The Cold Light of Dawn

The Moulding of a Man

To become enlightened you don't have to 'pass over', but it does provide a bit of reassurance that you are on the right track.

This is the incredibly uplifting story of a man who thought he was leading a pretty ordinary sort of life for fifty-five years - then had a life-changing experience, and spent the next three decades coming to terms with the consequences.

Hamish Miller is best known for his trilogy of earth energy travelogues, *The Sun and the Serpent (1989)* and *The Dance of the Dragon (2000)*, both co-written with Paul Broadhurst, and *In Search of the Southern Serpent (2006),* co-written with New Zealander, Barry Brailsford. Although he had several other titles to his credit, these three books have made him a living legend in dowsing circles and something of a cult figure in the wider alternative community.

But long before Hamish Miller became Britain's best known - and certainly best loved - dowser, he was, like the rest of us, just a kid. Growing up, getting older - but, in his own retrospective consideration, not getting much wiser. From the perspective of the new millennium, his youth seems anything but ordinary, but the insight brought about by his Near Death Experience (NDE) in 1982 made those early years look colourless in comparison with what was to follow.

For my own part, I was born in Southampton in 1951. George the Sixth was just about to pop his clogs - and the city was still pockmarked by burgeoning buddleia bombsites and surreal scrapyards of rusting and remaindered redundant US military hardware waiting for the totter's torch.

The style of town planning favoured by the Luftwaffe for my home city owed more to Attila than Abercrombie, but the gaps in the streets were being progressively filled by brash new buildings, all concrete and glass, some elegantly functional, others a little futuristic. Although I had no other perspective from which to judge it at the time, in hindsight, optimism and opportunism were everywhere.

A boy from Bo'ness

For the young Hamish, that stage of his life was spent growing up in inter-war industrial Scotland and such a post-apocalyptic, future fantasy landscape wasn't even on the semaphore (the RADAR having yet to be invented). His was a childhood of coal mines and coal miners, cobbled streets filled with children playing - a tough, working class town, where men were men, boys were boys and everyone knew who they were, where they came from and where they were going. It was a place of clear lines, sharp divides and an angular social order. In such a setting, even slight deviations from the accepted lot of the masses were viewed with a mixture of suspicion and resentment. In his own words:

> I was born in Bo'ness on the banks of the Firth of Forth. Robbie Burns described Bo'ness, very accurately, as *"that dirty, ugly place, Borrowstounness"*. In my youth, Bo'ness was a mining town, pure and simple. That made my early life quite difficult, because all the boys at the local school were the children of miners and I was regarded as a 'toff', because my father had a <u>car</u> and he was a dentist. So I got thumped regularly - not particularly bullied - but I developed an internal resistance to opposition. Looking back, I think this was really quite valuable.

Hamish (top) with his mother and sisters in THE car - 1930

> The sort of thing that happened was that when I was about 8 or 9, I got a bicycle - and not many of us had bicycles. One day I went to school on my bike and some kids came rushing up, spoiling for a fight. One of them said 'y'ur back wheel's goin' roond'. This was intended to be a serious insult, and I was supposed to get very uptight about it, but I just shouted back 'So's the front yin'. They got really furious about this and ran after me. I pedalled like mad and got out of the way. These were the sort of little things that were part of growing up there.

Not only were Hamish's school friends lacking in bikes, some were lacking in shoes.

Bo'ness today is an attractive part of the Edinburgh and Grangemouth commuter belt. But in the 1930's it was a thoroughly blackened town. Everyone owed their livelihood, even their very existence, to Old King Coal. Freighters would arrive at the docks (now a pleasant marina), laden almost to the funnels with pine-tree trunks, ready for use as pit props. Vessels would be loaded directly

**Ships in the dock at Bo'ness
in the early 1930's**

from wagons, which shed their huge loads of coal from upturned trucks directly into the holds of waiting ships. Clouds of coal dust were accompanied by the cacophonous noise of mineral on metal.

When Hamish was 6 or 7 years old, a dramatic innovation came to Bo'ness - pit head baths. Prior to that, miners would have had to trudge home, encrusted with the finest black gold, and then have to scrub themselves clean in a zinc tub in front of the fire. It was a time and a place where things really were, stereotypically, grim up north.

My early life could not have been more of a contrast. We ran a street corner shop in Southampton. As the turnover was too small to support any staff, other than a few paper boys (youngsters who delivered newspapers, not lads made of cellulose, you understand), my mother worked full-time alongside my father and (apparently) I spent a fair part of my babyhood sat on the counter, much to the delight of other local mums. It was a successful little shop, but the working days were long and hard, preparing Morning, Evening and Sunday papers. As no-one had bought me by the time I had reached four years old, the Twinn family relocated to the home that was to see me through the rest of my childhood years. By then, it was the mid-1950's. Harold McMillan, the Prime Minister, was telling us we'd Never Had It So Good and, in at least one sense, he was right. We arrived in Newbury, in what was then still quite rural Berkshire, and landed squarely on our feet on a smart, spacious, brand-spanking-new council estate with an impressive new state-of-the-art primary school, just opened, and a new lock-up shop by way of family employment. The window blind read Newsagent, Confectioner, Tobacconist in bold black capital letters. As the estate grew up around us, the trade in the shop grew apace. We acquired staff and ever more paper boys (it being illegal to employ girls at the time). Eventually we did so well, we were able to buy a new bungalow, just about within walking distance of the shop.

In hindsight, one of the remarkable things about this housing estate was the apparent absence of local people. We were just about all 'from away' - some further than others. There were people from Poland and Ireland, Jamaica and Czechoslovakia (as it was called then) - and people from all over the UK. As a Hampshire lad, I was almost on home turf. Yet at school, we never noticed this. We were just a bunch of youngsters of the same age, growing up in a world of apparent, and much appreciated, peace - and one of astonishing technological progress. Adult wages were good and the material comforts of even the most humble residents were greater than anyone could have considered possible a generation earlier. Who cared where you came from or which creed you followed?

The similar stage in Hamish's upbringing was a very different kettle of fish. It's quite difficult for soft suburban southerners like myself to fully appreciate what lowland Scotland must have been like in the run up to WWII.

> There was something we did then, that I didn't understand at the time. There was always a gang of us in the playground, and from time to time, somebody would say 'let's go and thump the papes'. We'd all join together, about 20 of us, and we'd rush over to the wall of another school, about 200 yards away. If there were more of them than there were of us, when we got there, then we would shout at them and beat a hasty retreat. But if not, then we would thump them and chase them down the road. It was years before I realised what the 'papes' were - they were Roman Catholics, obviously - but I didn't know that. The universal cry of 'thump the papes' received an automatic response.

Again and again in my numerous discussions with Hamish, the hard edges and gruff distinctions of his early life came to the fore. How you were expected to act, where you worked, even who you mixed with, were given, defined, and set in the societal wall of stone. Another profound element in the education of the young HM, that sets him a glen apart from 'baby boomers' like myself, was the differential treatment of the sexes.

My own early education was undertaken at John Rankin primary school - a model of new order modernity. Opened in 1954, by the then Education Minister, Sir William Penney, it was a place where competitiveness was merged with egalitarianism, as the class divide fudged into the increasingly prosperous sixties. Children in our upper years were seated according to their exam performance at the end of the previous term. In front of me sat those who had achieved higher scores - a boy next to a girl. As there were always more bright girls, some of them were seated together. I am sure that glass ceilings and female physiology cramped their opportunities somewhat in the years that were to follow, and consequently allowed moderately-talented youths, like myself, an unfair advantage. But doubtless most of those girls did go on to higher education and became unsung captainnes of society.

In the post-war household that shaped and nurtured the young Millers however, things were very different for women.

The Bo'ness Academy Parade, with Hamish the scout beside the car and his sister Kathleen as the Academy Queen - 1938.

I had two elder sisters who were much cleverer than myself. One had been Dux (exemplary student) of the school, and both had been successful sportswomen. I was expected to do what they had done - but I didn't. I didn't have the talent, that's the truth.

They always thought that I was the spoiled brat of the family, and in fact, they were probably quite right. I was the boy with the curly hair, and they were the two older girls with straight hair. I was always the white sheep.

My older sister was very bright intellectually, but my father said 'Girls get married, and it's not worth their going to

University'. This was, of course, absolutely absurd, because she was much brighter than I ever was. Just to get out, she joined the ATS and went into RADAR operation, when it came in first. It was highly technical stuff, but she had a natural bent for that sort of thing.

The serious business of growing up

Even if the young Hamish could have thought 'outside of the box' as we say today, he (and just about every other young person of the era) was hemmed in by expectation and classification. The sixties, the Beatles, the can-do generation and letting it all hang out were socially many light years and several galaxies away.

I was a good golfer when I was a kid, so I said to my father, I think I would like to be a professional golfer. He said 'You can't be a professional golfer, there's no money in it, there's no respectability, there's no this, there's no that'. It wasn't a profession. It was a move away from the normal disciplines.

My mother once asked me, 'What would you like to be?' and I said 'I want to be a blacksmith'. She said 'No, no, no, you must get a proper job'. I asked 'What's a proper job?' She replied that I should become a doctor, a dentist, or a civil servant. I asked 'What's a Civil Servant? - What do they do?' and she said 'I don't know, but it's a proper job'. So I said that I wanted to be an engineer, because I liked to use my hands to make things.

Even the developmental impact of this grim stratification pales into insignificance, when you start to understand the hidden baggage of HM's family background. Although we lived in the same Kingdom, and we were only separated in age by a couple of decades, it seems a planet, perhaps a dimension, away from my own childhood in the rolling hills and quiet residential areas of southern England.

I had a very strict father, who was heavily influenced by the Wee Free Church up in Caithness, which was pretty fierce. You know, they were almost excommunicated if they whistled on a Sunday. My uncle got into terrible trouble when he cycled to church one Sunday because he had a bad leg. He was ostracised for weeks. It was a strictly disciplined way of life, based around the family Bible, and the endless, endless, endless prayers every evening.

They were incredibly hard workers. They had 12 acres of land. Co-incidentally, I've got that now, here in Cornwall - but theirs was hard, unforgiving ground and they had to shift all the stones off it themselves. They developed a field of

corn and they had a few hens, a few sheep, and a cow. They fished for bait in the afternoon, baited the crab creels in the evening, and went back down in the morning to pick up the crabs. Then they carted them up the steps of a 300-foot cliff. The place was called The Whaligoe. They filled barrels with live crabs at the local station and sent them to London for 10 shillings a barrel. Of course the crabs were all crawling around in the barrels at the outset. When the load got to London, the buyers chastised the fishermen because the crabs had all

Whaligoe steps - Caithness

settled down and there was only two thirds of a barrel of them. It was a desperately hard life, but I think that perhaps that part of my heritage has given me a solid resilience.

My father was one of eight children ... from my fertile grandparents ... well, they hadn't much else to do in the croft, and they had big families. The eldest always went into the Ministry and others went into the army. Many of them were killed, actually, in the First War. My father didn't want to work on the farm; he didn't want to do the fishing. He saw an advertisement in the Wick Herald for a job as a dental mechanic, at half a crown a week. He got the job, and he worked as a dental mechanic for three years.

However, he decided he wasn't going to get anywhere that way. At that time, there was - and in fact, there still is - the availability of the Carnegie money, Scottish Carnegie grants. He got a grant to go to Edinburgh University to take up dentistry. He wanted to be a doctor, but they wouldn't give him a grant for the number of years he needed, so he became a dentist.

In the First World War he was a Royal Artillery man, and that had a profound effect on him. He only started to talk to me about his experiences in the First World War late in life. I took him on a nostalgic journey back to Scotland when he was 79. He just started to talk about his experiences then. I think he had kept them in, all his life, and that was why he was always kind of uptight.

Young Hamish with his father and sister

My mother was the giggler in the family. She was the outgoing one with a great sense of humour. She died of a heart attack when she was 65. My parents had just moved down to Bristol to retire, but sadly it didn't last very long. She was wonderful.

Whether or not you believe that people are made of clay into which the spark of the divine is added, like chilli to a pizza, there is little doubt that our early years and the events that lead up to our appearance in the world have a major part to play in our subsequent development.

We are like the dough of life, pummelled and kneaded by the energy of the world around us at the time. Long before we bake in the glare of societal sunshine, we acquire a gargantuan amount of baggage, which most of us spend the rest of our lives either sifting through and coming to terms with - or blanking out in vain denial.

Even for Hamish Miller, who later experienced events that effectively restarted the clock, some of his particular baggage could still be glimpsed poking through the thin veneer of a 21st century existence.

One of the first things that struck me about this allegedly ordinary upbringing was the sharp concentration - and the determination to succeed in everything he did. You read about such people in the papers, yet most of the lads I grew up with on our estate had little more ambition than to have an easy life - the antidote to their parents' endless treadmill of labour just to stand still and to keep their heads above water.

HM was clearly very different, even at an early age. Despite his assertion that he was a bit clueless, it is quite apparent that if he was to do anything at all, it was to be done properly.

Hamish the young golfer - about 1939

I started to play golf. I became very keen and I won the Under-12 county championship, which was quite big stuff in Scotland at that time.

I was also very keen on Scouting. I did a lot of activities with the scouts - and I became what was called a King's Scout. I was awarded a Bushman's Thong, with badges in woodcraft, camping, lighting fires and that sort of thing.

I became very interested in swimming. At about the age of 9 or 10, I used to get on the bike on a Saturday morning. The swimming baths were in Falkirk. Two or three of us used to 'catch the bus', which meant we rode behind the bus, which was quite a small bus, and we used to go in the slipstream and cycle the 7 miles up to Falkirk. We had a routine; we used to swim a mile, up and down, and then cycle back.

I then went to a school in Edinburgh, and was introduced to rugby. I was also in the golf team in the school. I really enjoyed competition.

Even away from his school life, his education continued to ground him in a very practical way, where achievement and reward were paramount:

On holidays from secondary school, I went to youth hostels and worked on Forestry Commission land. It was my first introduction to (a) a job where I earned some money and

(b) how the guys who were doing the job behaved towards those who were organising them.

This was new territory. The job was to get to the Forestry Commission hut by 07.00 in the morning, and to walk up about a mile and a half of wet grass slope to where they had planted little trees about two years earlier. The grass was 3 foot high - and the trees were about 6 inches tall. You had to crawl through the wet grass with a sickle and take all the grass out. The first few were marvellous, but by the time you had done it for a couple of hours . . .

We had a guy who was in charge of our squad. I never had a watch, but I used to get the idea that it was teatime and I would start to make my way back to the hut. He would start the journey slowly down from the hill and I would go down like a hare. He used to shout at me to come back, because he had calculated that he would be paid for walking down the hill very slowly and reaching the hut at the right time. He didn't want me haring ahead, because they would know we had stopped early. I started to understand this social blend of 'us and them', between workers and management. One time we were 45 minutes late coming down and I was furious that I had worked all that extra time and not been paid for it. I went in the next day and pointed out that I had worked 45 minutes over time - and they just pulled out a sheet that showed that on Monday I was 12 minutes late, on Tuesday I was 15 minutes late . . .

The next job I had was with an uncle of mine. During the war, timber was worth a fortune. He saw an opportunity, borrowed some cash and bought some woods further up in Scotland. He built a sawmill and started making pit props, larch beams for timber buildings and the like. I used to stay at his house, when I was 16 or 17, and work with him during the school holidays. I really learned. He was the boss - and I was a labourer in the sawmill.

The sawyers were on contract, and they kept going like the clappers, because they were only paid at the end of the day so much a cube for what they had cut. They were throwing great lumps of wood on to gantries. We labourers had to pick them up, lug them down the yard and stack them in the right place. Sometimes, it was icy in the yard, which made a tough job quite dangerous. When the belt came off from the mechanical saw from time to time, there were great cheers from us, because we knew we wouldn't have to carry anything for a while. But the sawyers soon got mad, because they weren't earning anything. I became very aware of the workplace dynamics - between the unskilled workers, the skilled workers and bosses. In later life, this experience was invaluable.

While his educational and early working life indicates a formidable and feisty youth, it was his sporting prowess that, more than anything, marked him out as a potential high-achiever:

St Andrew's University Swimming Team 1945/6 - Hamish top left

Later, I played at full back for both Heriot-Watt and St Andrew's University rugby teams - which I'm quite proud of, actually. I was in the swimming team at University as well, so I had a very active young life.

St Andrew's University rugby team 1945/6 - Hamish far left

I, too, played at full back - for the school hockey team, following in my mother's plimsoll prints - but this was very much an exception, in a comparatively quiet childhood. I was expected to keep out of trouble and keep my head firmly below the parapet. However, to HM, determination, concentration and success were the norm. Several decades and almost literally a lifetime away, the jovial, amiable and seemingly easy-going Miller was still just as focused as ever on what he wanted to achieve. The drive for self-betterment may have been replaced by the desire to help others, but the fire was still burning and the vision was still in sharp resolution.

When I started out on this quest to uncover the real Hamish Miller, I expected to come across elements of his young life that would have acted as a precursor to the dramatic change of attitude and outlook that came about as a result of the NDE. Yet, time and again, all I bumped up against was a hard headed, materialist ghost - in fact, just the sort of person that a long-haired dreamer from the Home Counties like myself would have avoided like the plague.

Out of your body? - what a load of Cobbler

Just one event indicated that, spiritually, the gritty Scot might not have been quite the same as most of the rest of us. It came during a teenage expedition to a mountain called The Cobbler in Arrochar. An inexperienced and ill-equipped group of youngsters took it into their heads to attempt to conquer this substantial peak in winter. It sounds the sort of venture that English urban youths today might translate into riding a motorbike at excessive speed without wearing a helmet.

The Cobbler - Painting by Neil Barlow

To cut a long story short (and it's covered in consummate detail in Hamish's 1998, somewhat premature, autobiography *It's Not Too Late*), HM fell off an ice-covered ledge and plunged 300ft to a certain death - except that he lived to tell the tale. Once in mid-flight, Hamish felt himself apparently leave his body and observed, with great clarity and some regret, the 'flailing rag doll' that was himself tumbling precipitously down the near-vertical scree. By an astonishing coincidence, if you still believe in such things, Hamish landed on the one piece of snow deep enough and soft enough to break his fall. He walked away with little more than skin damage and bruising. The escape was miraculous, but the out-of-body experience was portentous. We will return to this theme later in the story.

In the service of the King

Just about everyone of a certain age was obliged to do their bit during World War II. Most did so willingly, but with a mixture of trepidation and resignation about entering the fray in person. Not so the young Miller, the personification of the gritty Brit;

> I was excited about the prospect of getting into the war, because I wanted to be a fighter pilot. I volunteered, but I was only 15 and nine months, so they said 'come back in 3 months'. Then I wanted to join the navy. They offered me an engineering cadetship, but then they cancelled the scheme. I thought, to hell with that, I wanted to volunteer - but I thought I would go to university first.

HM's education was rudely interrupted, as it was for most young men of the time, by the intrusion of National Service. For most of us who have grown up in the long period of relative domestic tranquillity that was the last half of the twentieth century, it is sometimes difficult and uncomfortable to recall that, but for the chain of events that led to the involvement of the US in WWII, we could have spent this lifetime in an occupied land - if we had even had the chance to go round this cycle at all. Hamish only just missed being called up to active service, and all young men were still required to receive two years military training well into the 1950's. The coalition of allies may have defeated the Germans twice in a century, but there was no room for complacency. As if to add an even harder edge to HM's outlook on life, his experiences of the period were no cadet force joyride.

> I went into the army. I had some time in the Engineers as part of National Service. It was important to my development, because I went in not knowing how the other half lived at all.
>
> Straight from university, I was put into specialised training, because I was A1 fit. This unit was the precursor of the SAS - the Special Air Service it was called. I worked for a while with the Marine Commando section. Part of the training for this cadre was about how to kill people with little bits of stick. That lasted about six months. They reduced you to a creature that does exactly what he's told, without reason, because no doubt on active service you would expect to be put in circumstances where you couldn't survive any other way. They change your entire being.
>
> I hadn't realised that they had changed me so much. But at the end of the six months training - which was very, very hard - they said 'OK, you now have 48 hours leave'. We'd just been on one of those manoeuvres where you go 5 days with a little can of water and you're attacked by people from base camp and all that sort of thing - and I'd had about 4 hours sleep each night for 5 nights. Although we were given the leave to enable us to go to London, we still had to cart half of our gear with us.
>
> I soon realised how much they _had_ changed me. We'd had no sort of involvement with civilians during that time at all - for what must have been around 5 months. I walked into a tube train with some of this gear on, and wearing the uniform

- I was a squaddie - and as I walked down the middle of the corridor, this guy stuck his foot out. I didn't think at all, but I went into a complete attack mode. I had very hard hands and I was about to chop him down - but a fraction of a second before I did so, a little voice in my head said 'What have they done to you?' I pulled back just in time - but the effects of the training were quite shocking.

This training was cathartic and it had a profound effect on me as a person. It took me through a stage of - and this is not romanticising - from being a fairly gentle sort of guy to someone who was perfectly prepared to go for it, almost without reason.

Worse was to come. The ambitious and successful Miller returned to Edinburgh University after National Service to finish his interrupted degree studies. Unlike today, if you failed a part of the course, you failed - that was it.

At the end of the course, I failed the final paper on abstract mathematics - and that was a fairly important part of it. The additional maths you had to do wasn't really a subject; it was more an attitude of mind, actually. My mate, Ian Ross, was doing the same exam and he was in the same state that I was. I saw him sling his bag across his back - and he just walked out of the gym, where the exam was being held. I sat there and tried to do something with it, but I could make no sense of it. I failed that particular subject, and I did not get the degree.

Hamish (right) with Ian Ross

To be perfectly honest, I've never regretted it since, because I had such a wonderful time at university. I learned so much that was nothing to do with the course - and my golf didn't half improve! But my father was very disappointed, because he had set his heart on me having a degree of some kind. He was a degree man himself and I felt I was a huge disappointment to him.

The Business of Success

Hamish may not have completed his degree, but he had already learnt a lot about life that would stand him in good stead in the years ahead.

Generally electrical

He got a job with the American-owned conglomerate The General Electric Company (GEC), but progress was too slow for the ambitious Miller. If he wasn't to have a successful career in his homeland, perhaps he could make something of himself where the streets were, allegedly, paved with gold.

> I came down to England in 1953 to earn my fortune in London. I brought my prospective wife down with her father, and a very smelly old dog, and stayed in the Embassy Hotel in Bayswater Road. I think it cost us about five pounds a week for the three of us.
>
> I was immediately put on to looking after the Coronation decorations in Regent Street. I was the only one in England allowed to park my car in the middle of Regent Street. I had a 30 horsepower Ford V8 Drophead, which was quite something in those days. The Coronation decorations included six foot diameter pink roses - and they had to be taken up 120 foot ladders. I had a miraculous escape during that time.

Coronation decorations in Regent Street

We had real problems with the contracting company. They kept going out on strike every few days before the Coronation. These contractors said 'we will fix these decorations to the walls, but GEC must deliver them to us'. My nightmare was in Oxford Circus. There was a three or four stage ladder, going up to the fourth storey. The guys who were going to fix these six foot diameter roses were standing on a ledge at the top, and I was standing at the bottom. I said 'well here's your ...' and they said 'nah, we want them up here'. So, I started going up the ladder, with what was in effect a huge umbrella on my back. The ladder started to move in the wind and I was just about to be pulled off, when the guys who were on strike said 'Pack it up, pack it up. Go back down, we'll do it.' I was terrified, absolutely terrified.

The great irony of this little tale is that, having been through the fire to get these blinking decorations ready for the brief passing of Her Majesty, and having assured himself of a place in history and any number of pole positions from which to watch the spectacle, the legendary Illuminating Engineer was so tired that he slept right through it.

So that was the first job at GEC in London. I was a lighting man doing what they called Illumination Engineering; specifying the right lighting for factories and all that sort of thing.

I thought I would really like to get into the design of the lighting fittings because my area of work was very restricted, so I became a designer of lighting fittings for them, for a while.

However, shortly after that GEC bought the Sobell company - to get a chap called Weinstock who was their big white chief. GEC wanted to get him in as a hatchet man. They paid eight million at that time for the company, mainly to get this particular man. I feel he got a Title for destroying the lives of thousands of really loyal hard-working people, for creating huge problems for suppliers by extending the payment period from 30 days to 90 days and for selling off huge lumps of the company. The City thought he was wonderful. I knew his reputation beforehand and I realised that that was the time I should get out, because I knew something unpleasant was going to happen.

I went on to Philips to see what they were like, but it was still the same sort of job, so I thought, 'No, I'll go out on my own'. This is how the whole manufacturing business started - in a garage in Twickenham.

From employee to employer

With an engineering background, a practical approach to life and a 'can do' mentality, HM recognised a niche in the market and switched from designing light fittings to designing furniture.

I started designing small items of furniture. I had a workshop of my own; I used to make little candleholders and other bits and pieces. I realised pretty soon that I couldn't make a living out of selling candleholders; I needed to be producing decent sized pieces of furniture. So, we started making bigger and bigger items.

**Actress Rula Lenska
modelling one of
Hamish's chairs**

As the business grew, he moved from the one-man workshop in Twickenham to a bigger place in Findon, Sussex, employing 5 or 6 people. However, after a while the local villagers became concerned at the level of noise from the presses and the delivery lorries, so he moved the operation again, to a unit in the Tannery Yard in Steyning, Sussex, where he had about 10 employees.

After some while, I got to a point where I had a window reserved for me in Liberty's in London for the products we had made. Heals, which was quite a big furniture company in Tottenham Court Road, had my occasional tables. I was doing quite well on the design front, but I needed to make the items in larger quantities, and to the standard I wanted.

I couldn't get another manufacturer to make them for me, so I started my own manufacturing business.

I realised that if we were going to compete in the wider market, we had to have a sales rep. and other specialist staff. So, the business developed into something much larger and we moved to Smalldole.

With design that captured the mood of the moment, the much-vaunted furniture was soon rolling off the production line. Expansion was steady and sustained and by the 1970's there were nearly 100 people employed at the main plant at Smalldole, with another building nearby being used as a Headquarters.

Looking back, Hamish was clearly very satisfied with what he achieved in the world of business and manufacturing. His father was less enthusiastic.

Smalldole furniture factory - Sussex

I took my father round the factory - an all day tour of all the departments. We were making very modern, very upmarket, very trendy furniture, and we had a very efficient group of people doing it. At the end of the visit, I took him up to the boardroom. We had a large whisky and I asked him 'What do you think?' He had a big sip of his whisky; he paused for a minute and he said 'It's not what you started out to do'.

That was a cathartic moment for me, because I thought he would be quite proud of what we had built up - with the Jaguar car outside and all the trappings of success. But I realised then that maybe I wasn't doing the thing that I really wanted to do.

Remanence of a High-Roller

There are few people left alive who knew Miller The Main Man from his entrepreneurial heyday. Blood relatives apart, the one who does recall the flamboyant factory-owner is former family friend, and now his third wife, Ba:

> 'We lived in the same village as Hamish's family. They lived about two fields away, so I knew him quite well from the time when he had his factory. I remember that on one occasion my son and I were even taken on as staff to help in the packing department - working with the furniture coming off the conveyor belt. As a temporary job, I found it quite interesting, finding faster ways to do the packing. In the end, I got really proficient at it.
>
> When I knew Hamish in those days, he was always full of life. He used to give parties at his house, especially for clients like his Japanese buyers. He was the life and soul of the party. Everybody in the village loved him. I seem to recall that he was very fond of eating and drinking.
>
> I can clearly remember that one Christmas we were going around the village carol singing. Suddenly this great limousine came swooping round the corner and almost went into the ditch. Hamish jumped out and came over to join us. He was quite inebriated and sang the carols at the top of his voice. It was so typical of him then.
>
> He loved playing tennis and you would see him around the village, taking part in everything. But he was quite a lad! Women were quite attracted to him, which was doubtless good for his ego. He would wear expensive clothes - from Harrods. It was very much a high-rolling lifestyle.
>
> Although Hamish was such an affable man, the whole outlook of the better-off people in the area was all about one-up-man-ship, which I couldn't stand. It was all about dinner parties, and about out-doing other people's dinner parties. Hamish was very much involved in that kind of life at the time. He had little thought for . . . . well, it seems a long time ago now.'

Hamish the Smith

Whilst most of his time and energy was directed at running and building up his business, there was one aspect of his life that he found time to indulge. As we have already noted, when asked, at the age of six, what he wanted to be when he grew up, Hamish replied without hesitation - a blacksmith. He was fascinated by the sheer alchemy of turning lumps of metal ore into recognisable, usable objects. Amongst his staff at the Smalldole factory, was a man who was to help him to realise this childhood dream.

Hamish (left) and Bob Fawkes at the Smalldole factory

I discovered that my works director, John Lawson, had been a blacksmith, and his father had been a blacksmith before him. From time to time, we used to have a pretty cathartic reversal of roles. He used to come up on a Monday evening to my little forge, after I had pushed him the previous week to produce as much as we could get out of the factory. John used to come up, immaculate in a white collar and tie, and teach me blacksmithing. He would sit in a chair in a corner and for an hour and a half he would reduce me to a little black greasy spot. He would pick up whatever I'd made and say "Rubbish" and walk out. He was a great teacher, actually. That's probably why I'm now quite a good blacksmith. I used to harangue him when I came in on the Tuesday, and he would know perfectly well that I would do that. It was a brilliant way to learn.

It seems almost an innate act of grounding for those of us who spend endless hours cooped up in offices and factories to seek some kind of worthwhile physical activity to rebalance the energy dissipated so unnaturally sat at a desk and/or in front of a computer screen.

For Hamish, the actions of the blacksmith - the hot metal, the fire, air and water -remained a powerful draw all his life. Looking at the metalwork he created, both functionally and artistically, it is clear that there was a lot of the essential Hamish invested in his work. The dowsing rods he forged for me are a minor work of art.

He freely admitted that he took greater pride in being an effective blacksmith than he ever did in being an efficient businessman. He felt that it was a hugely respected profession and, even in his ninth decade, he was still an enthusiastic metal basher.

We will return to the quite remarkable output of Hamish's forge at the very end of this book.

Still Hopeful in Davy Jones's Locker

If there is a story anywhere in this section that sums up Hamish's determination to succeed in everything he did, it is the saga of the sinking of the Hopeful.

By the late 1970s, Hamish was earning a very good income and he was starting to look for a way to provide himself with a pension. Doubtless, you or I faced with a similar decision, would probably have stuck it in some sort of sensible, but unexciting, growth fund, or maybe just ploughed it back into wherever we were living at the time. Hamish decided to buy a fishing boat - and I don't mean one with oars.

> I already had a little fishing boat down in St Ives harbour. There was a yorkshireman called Pete Madden, who used to take it out with me in St Ives Bay, whiffing for mackerel. He did most of the fishing, but we split the income from the catch. One day, he suggested that we got hold of a bigger boat, so he could fish every day. This seemed a good idea, so we started looking around in the press. We discovered that there was a likely sounding vessel moored up in Scrabster, which was being sold by the Highlands and Islands Authority. Scrabster is a fishing town near John o' Groats, on the far north coast of Scotland.

The Highlands & Islands had put it on the market. Apparently various people had looked at it, but no-one had bought it, as it had a few obvious drawbacks. Two brothers had been fishing from it, but the year before, they had had a monumental row about the fact that one of them hadn't been paying his National Insurance. They had just walked off the boat and had never spoken to each other again. Their boat, the Hopeful, was lying at the quay, exactly as they had left it.

I went up to have a look and I just fell for her - her shape was quite beautiful. It was made by Millers of St Monance, who built larch on oak fishing boats - and they were absolutely gorgeous.

From the previous year, it still had some of the fish they had caught on their last voyage in the hold - and not surprisingly the smell had seriously put people off buying the boat. It had literally just been left as it was. It had an exhaust pipe, which came up vertically from the engine down below, which had a metal cap on the top to keep the rain out. In the haste of the previous owners to get away from one another, they had left the cap open and, of course, the rain had poured in. You don't have to come from Caithness to know what the weather is like in winter in the north of Scotland. Water had got down into the engine and into the cylinders - they were ruined. It was a complete pig in a poke and nobody with any sense would have thought about putting up the money to fix it.

But I really loved the idea of sailing her and, eventually, I managed to knock the price down because of the state she was in. I came to an agreement with the Highlands and Islands on a price, but my part of the deal was that I had to put her right and get her out of the harbour.
So, we cleaned her out and we got some local people to strip the engine down. An amazing crowd seemed to materialise just at the right time to help us to get her seaworthy again. We pulled the engine out on to the quayside and we put tarpaulins over it. There was a wonderful guy with a big golden earring and a very old Rover, who was a very good engineer. He would turn up in this old Rover with half a deer in the back, which he was swapping for something else - as they do up there.

Dounray, the prototype nuclear energy electricity generating station, was just along the coast. Whenever I said that I needed a bit of stainless steel to do this or that, the locals would say 'we'll do a Dounray on it'. It seemed to be part of their way of life - I got the impression that half of the fishing boats in the area had parts made out of bits from Dounray. Anyone with a family history that includes the Devonport Dockyard or the shipyards on the Clyde will be familiar with this scenario.

Eventually, we got the Hopeful put back together and we set sail with a depth sounder, a borrowed life raft and some very, very basic charts - the sort of maps you get in a schoolboy's atlas. We left Scrabster on a Friday. For reasons that we discovered to our cost later, in Scotland, you shouldn't set off in a boat or on a fishing trip on a Friday. In hindsight, the whole undertaking was absolute madness.

However, we made good progress round Cape Wrath, through the Minches, past Kyle of Lochalsh and across to the Island of Islay. We were held up in Islay for two or three days, which wasn't too tough an assignment, as all there is on Islay is a village and five distilleries.

Eventually, we did get across to Northern Ireland, and we sailed into Belfast. It was at the time when the IRA was active there, and as we sailed into the harbour the police were all round us, wondering what on earth we were doing. Later, we sailed on down the Irish coast, into Dublin, and then on towards Rosslaire in southeast Ireland.

By the time we were approaching Rosslaire, there was a gale warning in force. It was getting on for nine o'clock at night and darkness was imminent, but we could see the lights of Rosslaire harbour quite clearly. There was a great swell in the Irish Sea and there was clearly a big storm brewing, but given how close we were to the end of that leg of the journey, we thought we were pretty well home and dry.

However, about a mile and a half outside the harbour, we went up on the top of a wave crest and we came down very hard. The boat suddenly stopped - dead. After a few seconds, she rose up again and she started surging forward. So, we shrugged and thought no more about it - and we gunned it to get into the safety of the harbour. We hadn't travelled very far when my colleague, Pete Madden, went down below and shouted back up 'we've got a great big hole in the boat and the water's pouring in'. We stood there, transfixed, with the boat taking in all this water. There was very little we could do.

The Hopeful

Just before we'd left Scrabster, I'd rung Salvus Bain, the marine insurers. I told them that we were just about to take the Hopeful out of the harbour and sail her down to Cornwall. The man I spoke to said he knew the boat, so when I asked if he would insure her for me, please, as we were leaving the following morning, he said it would be all right. There was no time to exchange any of the paperwork, but the north of Scotland is a very laid back sort of place and it didn't seem to matter at the time.

Thankfully, on the recommendation of the fishermen in Scrabster, I had bought a good ship-to-shore radio as a safety device. With the water pouring into the hull, I checked the radio for the first time, and thankfully it was working. So, there we were, a mile and a half outside Rosslaire harbour, with a gale warning, the sea getting up and the water coming up to the gunnels. The water came up past the engine.

Needless to say, it stopped - and no amount of persuasion would restart it.

When we only had about 6 or 9 inches of freeboard left, and we were drifting, we had to accept that we would need to be rescued - with some haste. So, I cracked out the maroons (a sort of safety "rocket" to alert the coastguard to a ship in danger). It sounds so stupid now, but I had never looked at them before. A maroon is a sort of firework, so I got the matches out, lit the end and I held it in anticipation. Never having fired one before, I had no idea that a maroon takes about 5 or 6 seconds to ignite, before it takes off. So, after about 3 seconds I looked down at it to see what was wrong - and it whooshed up, missing my face by just a couple of inches. How it missed me, I have no idea. It flew a few feet above the sea and dropped in. So I fired another one.

I was starting to get the feeling that we really could drown if we didn't get help very soon, so I called Rosslaire harbour on the ship-to-shore radio and I explained, as calmly as possible, that we were the Hopeful and that we were about to sink. I asked them to raise the lifeboat urgently. To raise a lifeboat in Ireland at quarter to ten on a Saturday night was very difficult, because all the lifeboat men were in the pub. They were not insured to go out in the lifeboat, unless there are at least four qualified crewmembers - and they could only raise two. So there was quite a delay.

After what seemed like an age, I got on to the radio again, repeated the call and said, not so calmly, that we were sinking very fast and could they please do something about it - now. A voice came back from the radio at Rosslaire harbour, in a wonderfully strong dark Irish accent, and it asked 'Where are you then?' I replied that I could see all the lights of the town; that we were about a mile outside the harbour and that we had the mast lights and all the other lights on the boat blazing away.

After a slight break, he came back with 'I can't see you'. I was starting to get nervous and spluttered 'Well, how can't you see me - we're only a mile outside your harbour?' 'Ah' he replied, 'there's a bloody great wall between me and the sea'. In complete exasperation I said 'Well why don't you climb up the f****** wall and have a look!' In hindsight, it was hilarious - but we were about to drown.

By some miracle, the coastguard had picked up my message somewhere in Wales and they managed to get the lifeboat out to us in time. Even then, I was still keen to get the Hopeful into a port, so I suggested to the lifeboat coxswain that I would steer her, if he could pull us in. He explained that they were not allowed to do that, but that they could attach a rope and try to tow her into the harbour.

We had lugged this whacking great heavy life-raft on to the lifeboat, because it belonged to somebody else. It was the only thing we managed to get off her. The lifeboat towed her so far, but the rudder was snaking about all over the place and they got to the stage where they felt it was dangerous to tow it any further as it might have done something unfortunate to the lifeboat itself - so they had to cut the rope. I watched my pension, with all its lights on, gradually sinking into the Irish Sea. I watched it sadly until it was sitting on the seabed, 60 feet under the water. I'll never forget that moment.

The lifeboat crew were marvellous. They took us into the harbour and they asked us if we would like a suit (presumably of dry clothes). I wasn't in the mood to worry about my attire, so I replied that I didn't want a suit. Then they took us to the pub and brought us some foaming pints of Guinness. They said 'Aren't you lucky?' I replied 'What do you mean, lucky, we've just lost our boat!' 'Yes' they pointed out 'but you are still alive aren't you'. They made sure we were all right and got us some accommodation. It was absolutely astonishing - they were great.

Although it became a great after dinner story, there had been a real possibility that they would have died that night, because if the forecast weather had come in as expected they would have been in serious trouble. As it was, the storm came in two or three hours after the lifeboat took them off.

While we were recovering, a guy in the bar asked me if I wanted to get the boat up. I had no idea it would be possible, but he said 'I can get it up for you' and he offered to do it for £1,000. His plan was to fill it with air bags and, as it was a wooden boat, it would be OK. Eventually, that's exactly what he did. They got her up on to the shore on a very high tide, where we found that one of the planks had been neatly taken out just below the water line. It was a plank about 8ft long, 9 inches wide and about an inch thick.

We later discovered that about 40 years previously there had been a dredger called The Slaney, which had sunk in the bay with its bow pointing upwards. No-one had got around to salvaging her, so the authorities had put a protective basket on top of the tip of the sunken bow, with a buoy on top of that. The buoy had fallen off at some stage and had not been replaced - leaving the unmarked spike of angle iron, three feet below the surface of the water. Four decades after the wreck, we had come down on to it very neatly - I thought it was a superb bit of intuitive navigation. We had sailed 700 miles and I had managed to spear the tip of this wreck neatly with the bottom of our little boat. The iron spike had pierced the hull and it had just pulled out a plank. As the next wave lifted us off again, the water just surged in. I had a huge altercation with Irish Lights about this, but to no avail.

The following day, I rang Salvus Bain, the insurers. I explained that I was Hamish Miller of The Hopeful and asked, more in hope than expectation, if they remembered that I'd had a telephone conversation with them about 7 days previously, just before we left Scrabster. 'Oh yes, oh yes', the man replied. I told him that she had sunk - and I just wanted to check whether she was insured. To my great surprise and relief, the man said 'Oh yes, we'll honour that conversation'. So, I had the means then to pay the guy his £1,000 for lifting the Hopeful from Davy Jones's Locker and for getting the engine back in working order.

She was raised on to the shore and we put a temporary patch on her to keep the water out, because we'd had the engine stripped, repaired and re-installed. The local seamen found a long larch plank, which was thick enough to be curved in the right way. I asked the man who had lifted the boat up with the balloons if he knew a good ship's carpenter. He replied without hesitation that 'The fella' that's working on the roof over there is an expert'. As happened time and time again during this saga, the right person seemed to make an appearance just when I needed them. The fella' came down from the roof and, after a cursory conversation, he inspected the plank and he pronounced that 'it'll do'.

A couple of days later, he took out the temporary patch, just as the tide was going out. Then he started whittling away and shaping the replacement larch plank. The tide went all the way out - and then it started to come back in. I had this sudden dread that the reconditioned engine was about to be inundated with salt water all over again. The carpenter was sitting there, cross-legged whistling and whittling away until the incoming tide came practically up to his knees. In what seemed to be the nick of time, he dropped in the new plank and caulked it into place. It fitted perfectly first time - and it's never been touched since. Years later, I talked to the man who owns the Hopeful now, and he said he'd always wondered why there was that strange bit of planking just below the water line.

Eventually, we brought her over to Cornwall and we did do some fishing down here, but the fishing wasn't good enough to pay the harbour dues. So, we took her back to Peterhead in Scotland, to try to do some fishing there - but it didn't pay there either. Even after all of our best efforts, my pension idea was looking a bit sick.

However, I remembered that on the way down, at Ullapool in North West Scotland, we had tied up beside a little fishing boat, which was like a miniature version of the Hopeful. My boat was about 35ft long, whereas the smaller one was only about 23ft, but built by the same people. The owner had said to me at the time that if I ever wanted to sell that boat, he'd love to have it. So, I rang him up from Peterhead and asked if he still wanted it - and he rang The Highlands & Islands Authority, who bought it for him. We got most of our money back, so it didn't cost a great deal in the end - but it was the most incredible experience.

As I listened, it was hard not to think that there was a quite separate book waiting to be written around this remarkable story of endeavour and foolhardiness. It sums up so much of the man - and so many of the themes that we shall return to later. The serial survivor, the acceptance of the extraordinary as quite normal, the determination to achieve, repeated instances of synchronicity, the sense of being guided - and the ability to laugh at even the most traumatic of events, which others might have repressed forever.

From peak to trough

It wasn't just his fishing boat that rose and fell with the waves. Even bigger events were about to unfold. By 1980, HM was amongst the highest earning and best-regarded businessmen in the country. So much so that later in the year he was due to be lauded at a reception at the House of Commons as a shining example of enterprise in action. However, he never received his award - as the enterprise in question suddenly imploded. Like the premature dropping of a theatre stage curtain, the recession of 1980/81 put a sudden halt to the expansion of the business. In a world where just about every business exists on credit obtained from the banking system, when the good times stop rolling and the credit is called in, even the most efficient of enterprises is vulnerable. In hindsight, HM feels he was naïve in assuming that his financial providers were playing by the same rules, but when you have never experienced a recession before . . .

> I had a huge altercation with Barclays Bank at that time. I had just insured the factory for half a million pounds and there was more than a quarter of a million pounds worth of equipment in it, which we had built and paid for. Barclays took me out for the repayment of a loan of £73,000 - ironically, because we had given them too much information. We had prepared cash flows for the forthcoming financial year, for the next three years in fact, which gave them all the information they needed to decide to reduce their exposure to any potential default. If we had played our cards closer to our chest, we might have survived.
>
> It felt so unfair, because during the recession we didn't have a single order cancellation - although we had to extend our delivery times to meet our customers' needs. The man from the bank coldly stated "We are reducing our facility Mr Miller", which effectively ended any further hope of expansion and left us working hand to mouth, with a very tight cash flow. I said to them "How does that fit with Maggie Thatcher's proclamation about having tender care and

concern for British businesses?" They replied "We are having tender care and concern about our money, Mr Miller, not yours". Was it ever thus.

Anyway, that was the big change. For two or three years I had been pretty unhappy. Just to keep the factory going, I had to make less and less of the quality goods, and we were down to churning out television stands, television legs and television cabinets. I was using natural resources to produce stuff for the sake of producing it, just to survive. I didn't like that. Eventually, the bank called in their debt and wiped me out.

For all the bitterness and anger that lingered long after the collapse, you can't help thinking that Barclays actually did HM a big favour. It was a part of his life that had run its course. Yet, blacksmithery apart, it was the only way he knew of earning a living.

He struggled to keep the factory afloat, for the benefit of the workforce as much as anything, for as long as he could. He rightly took some pride and comfort from not having laid off his employees during the recession - although he wryly admitted that that probably added to the financial problems of his firm. For a man who had invested so much time and effort in the creative design of his products, it was clearly galling to have to spend the vast majority of his working life 'dealing with people and their problems' and, as subsequent events have shown, he was well off out of it.

Even after the final collapse, he had aspirations and opportunities to get back into the rat race. For all its mindlessness, the adrenalin rush of the business world can be a powerful addiction.

The powers that be, however, had other ideas.

Part Two

The Heat of the Day

To die, or not to die, that is the question

Many apologies to William Shakespeare, if he is still floating about, but hopefully Hamlet is out of copyright by now and can be sampled with impunity.

It is too late

One Wednesday in May 1982, the end of the world - or at least the end of a worldview - arrived. Hamish suffered serious physical pain in his stomach and chest and, having had little experience of, and even less time for, ill-health in his busy business life, he reluctantly decided to call a doctor. By that Sunday, Hamish was on the operating table being treated for acute diverticulitis and, seven hours later, was left there - for dead.

Hamish furnished the details in his own inimitable style in *It's Not Too Late*, but the scene was set for a second out-of-body experience. He distinctly remembers watching the surgeon and his colleagues scrubbing down after the regrettably unsuccessful operation, and heard the main man saying 'Pity we were too late, chaps'. Too late, TOO LATE, too late for what - lunch, the bus, Coronation Street? Gradually the reality of the situation started to sink in. His inner self floated around the operating theatre, while the medical team made their way off to fill in the paperwork, inform the body snatchers and go out into the fresh air at the end of their shift, feeling a bit disconsolate. HM too made his leave, without fear for the future, without regret for leaving his home or his loved ones behind - and without the slightest idea about where he was going.

A theme of this book is to try to explain in words what is well beyond textual description, so this section of the story needs to be considered as, at best, an interpretation of the actual phenomenon.

To make any sense of this part, we have to loosen the shackles of rationalism, at least of the kind defined by Descartes and his successors. What lies beyond the veil of this cycle of life has fascinated and frightened humankind since the dawn of time - and possibly long before that. Putting the idea of the hereafter into words has frequently led to some schismatic scriptural misinterpretations that have set culture against culture and philosophy against philosophy - with disastrous results on a global scale. We shall try to avoid that scenario here.

Not having been there myself yet, I am only the good scribe seeking to make sense of the incomprehensible - and then to convey it to a wider audience. What I can say is that whatever Hamish experienced, it changed him forever. Whether anything of his experience can truly be conveyed in words is problematic, but I am convinced that his enlightenment was the result of a real phenomenon - and that the implications of it are absolutely profound for both the way we live, and for the way we interact with this world - and potentially many other worlds.

Open your mind and your heart and see what you make of it . . .

Up the tunnel

As the 'reality' of the operating theatre dissolved away, a kind of virtual tunnel manifested itself, to which he was guided. He entered it and he 'became' what seemed to be a small tube with rounded ends within that tunnel. For what could have been a nanosecond or several hours he relocated into the tunnel and flowed with it until he reached a place like no other he had ever even thought he might experience.

> When I got to the end of the tunnel, there was absolute peace. I was very curious, but I had absolutely no fear at all. I'm not making a big issue of it, I just had no fear.

Hamish's Tunnel

When the tube stopped, there was a warm welcoming light. As I got out of the tube, it seemed as if I was a little babe. I think it must have been a representation of total innocence.

The Management

Once out of the tunnel, Hamish became aware that he was not alone. Trying to explain the nature of the other entities that were also in the place he had reached pushes the English language beyond its recognisable boundaries. As we talked, the frustration played out in his voice and his body language. It was so important to try to explain to the people that surround him what lies beyond, or within, the everyday world, yet there are no words to describe it and precious few concepts in which to convey it. If you try to crystallise the forms he encountered into common speech, you just end up sounding like a nutter - it's so . . . so . . . you know. The best he could do was to think of a new word; a word that avoided as much as possible of the baggage and the misconceptions of other ways of expressing the non-physical, the esoteric, the divine. He came up with the idea of calling them The Management.

> When you meet The Management, you can't see them. You're just aware of their communication. They 'said' 'These are some of our perceptions. If you can contribute to these, or even understand them, you're welcome to come in'. The only one that I can bring in that could give the faintest whiff of what it was about was the idea of 'the colour of music'. Now, it seems absolutely basic, simple, but it hadn't occurred to me that music had a colour at all. But of course it has - with a spectrum of different frequencies. If you apply the idea of 'the colour of music' to every subject that you can get your mind around, that's the kind of quantum leap of increase in perception I was exposed to. It was absolutely mind-blowing.

His impression was of somewhere that was unimaginably vast, but not disturbingly so; of being in a timeless dimension; of being somewhere all-knowing and totally benevolent. He sensed he was in the company of other entities, who might once have been 'people' as we know them. These entities, however, through some form of 'personal development', had found, been given directions to, or bought a ticket for the escalator to nirvana.

> I feel everyone is gradually edging towards having a bigger part in the process of creation. It's as simple as that. The entities I encountered seemed to have reached an advanced stage, but in essence, I think they were people like us, but at a higher level, if I can use such a simplistic concept. Maybe they're not just at the next level up, but possibly a couple of levels beyond that. They have become 'the receptionists in the anteroom', if you like.

I asked Hamish if he felt they were 'St Peter' figures, guarding the gates and judging those who sought entry? I was clearly being a bit tongue-in-cheek, given his anathema to scriptural dogma. However, Hamish was well aware of the gravity of the concept and thought long and hard before replying in his usual irreverent style:

> Well, maybe it's something like that -
> but there ain't any gates.
>
> However, I certainly got the feeling that you have to 'qualify', to have raised your energy level, or to have become enlightened to some extent, to be of any use at the next stage. But I don't think there's any way you can define that degree of qualification; it's an entirely intuitive self-judgement. When you are given the choice, you know if you've reached the required level to progress - and if not, you decide to come back and evolve further. In human terms, that can be a very, very long process, but in a dimension where time is of no consequence . . .

The Near Death Experience

To fully understand the context of Hamish's experience, we need to consider the wealth of information now available on this still taboo, yet astonishingly widespread, phenomenon.

There are many books, indeed whole websites, dedicated to the research and cataloguing of NDEs. They span continents and philosophies, a vast spectrum of cultures and outlooks - and aeons of time. Until I started this book, I had hardly <u>heard</u> of anyone having an NDE, and certainly never come across anyone in person; now it seems that just about everyone has had one - well, at least they know somebody, whose neighbour's aunt might have had one. It's so much more common and so widely, academically, medically documented that it must be one of the larger members of the herd of elephants in the room of modern science.

Like myself, Hamish had never heard of anyone who had enjoyed or endured an NDE prior to his own experience of the phenomenon and he had never even heard of it as a concept. Being the hard-nosed materialist that he was up to 1982, he freely admitted that if anyone had floated the idea with him, he would probably have uttered a number of rude words and laughed a lot.

Although what we might now refer to as NDEs are described in both the old testament of the Christian Bible and in *The Republic*, by the Greek philosopher Plato, the study of NDEs really only got underway in the modern sense of the word in the mid 1970s. When Dr. Raymond Moody's *Life after Life* was first published in 1975, it caused a sensation. It was the first serious study of the NDE phenomenon and it has sold millions of copies. Later that century, Dr. Kenneth Ring took up the baton and his book *Life After Death* was similarly highly controversial, but spectacularly successful. This was the first attempt to carry out a survey of large numbers of NDE survivors in a statistically scientific manner. He identified common features of the experience and took a rigorous, rationalist approach to documenting the mystery. Since then, the best-known writer on the subject has been P.M.H. Atwater. She has written numerous books, has a lively website and has studied the accounts of over 2,000 adult and nearly 300 child experiences. Her *Big Book of Near Death Experiences* is a remarkable compendium of both the history and the latest understanding of the subject. So widespread is interest in NDEs, that the International Association of Near Death Studies has been established to support and counsel those involved, whilst providing information and scientific data for those investigating the occurrence.

A couple of well-documented surveys have indicated that around 5% of the adult population of the US have had an NDE of some description. Initially, I was seriously surprised and somewhat sceptical of this figure. However, when you consider that it probably isn't the kind of subject that you would wade into over a pie and a pint in the pub, the number of friends and acquaintances you could discuss such a topic with dwindles considerably. If I have, say, 20 - 30 people in my immediate circle with whom I could broach such an issue, then the fact that I have known one NDE survivor - Hamish Miller - is about par for the course.

Perhaps the most significant themes that come out of the highly-charged episode in the lives of all of those who have been through it are:

- that there is a surprising degree of commonality in the descriptions - both of the transition and the destination - given that many, if not most, of the participants had had no previous warning of even the possibility of such an event, and

- that the experience changes their lives irrevocably; in most cases opening them up to a more holistic and benevolent outlook; a life largely free of fear, greed, desire and hatred. Some become ascetic monks or fearless evangelists of their chosen or given philosophies, while others, like Hamish, just stop being grasping materialists and embark on a renewed life of generosity, discovery and wonder.

A very few, understandably, can't hack it at all and just go mad, but whatever it is they see and sense, it certainly has a profound effect. If there is another plane of existence, it's certainly not a pale shadow of this one.

Another baffling aspect of the NDE episode is that few, if any, of those who experience the phenomenon suffer permanent brain damage. Normally, when a person dies medically, oxygen to the brain is shut off as the respiratory and circulatory systems cease to function. Five minutes without oxygen is usually as much as a human brain can stand without serious consequences. With NDE survivors (and as we have seen above, there are large numbers of these) there can be periods of 'death' much longer than this - sometimes up to an hour or more - and yet those reporting an NDE under such circumstances rarely appear to display any such symptoms. Hamish, who was out for the final count for between 15 and 30 minutes, depending on when you consider 'death' to have begun, argues strongly that his mental ability and clarity were actually enhanced by the experience. The NDE is clearly something that is operating outside of the current medical and psychological paradigm - an issue to which we will return later.

NDEs seem to happen primarily to those who, paradoxically, have had no previous spiritual interest or experience. This would certainly have included the materialist Miller. The textbooks on the subject seem to imply that those who have already opened the door to spirituality are less likely to be susceptible to the need of the lightning bolt delivered by the NDE. It is also interesting to note in this context that while the nonspiritual become more esoteric, those who might once have had some connection to an established religious persuasion tend to drift away from their formal practice towards a broader based view of both this world and the next.

Another factor common to those in the various studies is that NDE participants generally did not take, or at least were not under the influence of, drugs at the time of the occurrence. Many medical and recreational drugs tend to induce hallucinations, but seem to be something of a deterrent to the unfolding of the experience. While HM had never taken drugs, other than the odd wee dram, he was certainly under a general anaesthetic when he passed over, which is not surprising given the surgery that was being undertaken on him at the time. It is worth noting that in recent years the strength of the anaesthetic used in cases of major surgery has been increased to prevent the incidence of patients regaining consciousness during the process. Apparently, this has coincided with a decline in the incidence of NDEs reported during medical interventions of this type.

Thorough and fearless as ever, HM tried an experiment to see if the presence of anaesthetic could indeed have been a reasonable explanation of what had happened to him. During a subsequent operation Hamish established that he was to be given the same type of anaesthetic. On his way into the netherworld of painlessness, he determined to make a sortie down the tunnel again - after all, it had been such a wonderful experience on the previous occasion. It had changed his understanding of life completely. A quick visit, to let them know he was getting things sorted out now and to pick up a few tips on the next steps on the road to enlightenment. But . . . nothing. Not the faintest trace of The Management. Whilst this can hardly be described as a rigorous, controlled, scientific study, it may indicate that anaesthetic, even with those more susceptible to otherworldly transition, is not the complete answer.

People most likely to experience an NDE include those who have lost all hope of survival. Hamish's own view is that one of the critical factors was his certainty of physical death. During his out-of-body experience on the Cobbler, he knew he was about to die and esoterically pressed the button on the ejector seat. When he was rushed into hospital for his abdominal operation, he may have sensed at some level that this was a life-threatening situation - and by the time of the NDE, his medical team had - quite literally - given up the ghost. But on the pre-meditated trial, he knew he was not in any real danger. It was elective, preventative surgery.

However, set against that theory, and whilst on National Service, Hamish was the witness to a death, where the person concerned seemed to give no indication of being anywhere but present at the moment of his demise.

> There was one occasion when I was with the SAS that we were watching a demonstration by the paratroopers. The instructor explained to his men what they had to do if their main parachutes didn't open. 'All you have to do is to discipline yourself and do all the right actions.' He went up in an aircraft to 2,000 feet to demonstrate. He jumped out as planned - but his parachute failed to open. We watched him doing all the things he had said during the training that they would have to do. You could see all these movements going on. But 100 feet from the ground, he let out the most terrorised scream I've ever heard. I can remember it as clear as if it was yesterday. I wondered then about the out-of-body experience, because he screamed until he hit the ground. I don't think if he had come out of his body that he would actually have made that noise right up to the last. So, I'm not sure if it happens every time - or if it happens for everybody. For me, I certainly came out of my body. I was convinced I had no chance at all.

Another issue of great importance in connection with NDEs, is that people can tend to find the otherworld they expect, or can at least recognise - so Christians find Heaven, Buddhists Nirvana and doubtless pagan Norsemen the victorious banqueting hall of Valhalla. It could be argued that for a practical atheist like HM, a dimension populated by formless beings using unimaginably advanced technology would be just the sort of non-scriptural, non-denominational future he could cope with. You could also argue that, as it seems well nigh impossible to express the experience in worldly words, the place that Hamish visited could be interpreted to fit just about anyone's idea of what the next destination might be like - if they had ever had a mind to think about it at all.

> Absolutely. The descriptions of what happens at the other end of the tunnel vary depending on where people are coming from. For many, there's Jesus or Mary or Michael - or something that's been drilled into them for a long time. There was absolutely nothing of that in my experience at all.

> There were just beings that were of a higher level. They
> didn't need a body, they had a mind. They understood totally
> about my confusion. They were people I admired
> enormously. They were so knowledgeable about every
> thought that I was having. They could almost predict what I
> was going to ask. It had probably happened to them 40
> billion times before and I could imagine them thinking to one
> another 'Look out, here's another one coming in . . .'. But
> there was such certainty there, Nigel, that I can't emphasise
> strongly enough. It wasn't like a dream.

I joked with Hamish that his description of the tunnel made of high-tech 'aluminium' plates, 'riveted' together at the corners, could be interpreted as a furniture designer's take on the interface - something that others might see as a flaming chariot or as a moving staircase. Describing the indescribable leaves a lot of scope for florid expression.

However, one of the elements significant in most NDEs is that the clarity of the experience is quite different to the distortion and transience of the dream world. NDEs, almost without exception, are crisp, meaningful and personal.

Atwater states that, although there is a series of factors that are common to the vast majority of cases, in practice, no two experiences are identical. Each person applies his or her own expectation, baggage and interpretation to an experience, which universally defies the ability of vocabulary to explain.

During a survey carried out by Linley, Bryan and Conley in Washington in 1981, it was found that, of people who had undergone an NDE episode:

    75% experienced serenity
    71% experienced an out-of-body experience
    38% experienced a tunnel
    56% experienced seeing a light
    35% entered an inner setting

As we have seen, Hamish went through each of these stages.

In addition, of the generally accepted attributes of any 'genuine' NDE, Hamish experienced the following:

- Heard others say that he was dead
- An out of body experience
- No thoughts for those left behind
- Entered a tunnel
- Emerged into light
- A sense of awe, wonder, calm, serenity and love
- An awareness of other beings
- A full knowledge of his memories (often called a full-life review)
- Felt the release of stress
- Lost all fear, particularly of death
- Underwent a complete change of attitude to life
- Lost contact with most of those who knew him prior to the NDE
- Developed an interest in spiritual matters (where there was very little previously)
- Experienced a determination to actively help the wider community
- Developed a positive, selfless approach to life
- A yearning to return to the 'other world'
- Discovered an appreciation of joy and laughter

Apparently, it is also quite common for participants to become 'aware of invisible energy fields and auras'. So, from that perspective, Hamish's subsequent experience was pretty mainstream for this marginal world.

Given the implications for the current scientific paradigm, the attitude of the establishment has wavered between denial and ridicule. Yet, clearly a growing number of events are being documented and described - and a vast library of information is being compiled. There are many well-authenticated examples of medical staff and other hard-nosed professionals, such as Hamish himself, who have been through the fire and come back beaming.

If, like myself, you have either never heard of this phenomenon, or have lumped it into the category of 'wacky', along with ley lines and ghosts, I suggest that, while your mates are off playing golf, line-dancing, or whatever, you have a quiet look at one of the more respectable websites on the subject (such as that of the IANDS) and come to your own conclusions. You might be a bit surprised at what is generally known and comprehensively recorded. Perhaps more importantly, if you have a reasonably open mind, you may be more than a little interested in what it might mean for your own prospects.

As a footnote to this pivotal point in the life of Hamish Miller, I too nearly died - almost before I had begun. On Coronation day in 1953, while Hamish was asleep, after working himself into a lather in a foreign land called London, I would have been waving the standard issue paper Union Flag somewhere on the roadside in Southampton. It's not that I've ever been a great patriot or royalist but, at 18 months old, you don't get over-concerned about such niceties. In time-honoured fashion I got tired of waving this wooden stick about and stuck it in my mouth, as you do - and then proceeded to fall over. My father may have known nothing of first aid, let alone medical best practice, but he did have indispensible native Geordie common sense. Without question, his prompt action of lifting me upside down by my legs and allowing the blood to flow out through my mouth, until it stopped of its own accord, saved my life. I don't recall seeing any tunnel, lights or multi-dimensional beings, but maybe I wasn't destined to get out of it all that early - or that easily!

Back for more punishment

Having spent a surprisingly brief period in this peaceful paradise, Hamish chose to rejoin us. In our discussion, we talked at some length about why he made this seemingly incomprehensible decision.

Desperately applying logic to a patently alogical situation, I suggested that he might have been sent back as a misplaced member of a mutant sub-species, but apparently the attitude of The Management is rather more humane than that. I also proposed that he might have chosen, as a suddenly enlightened being, to return like a Buddhist bodhisattva or a born-again Christian Saint, to help his blinkered fellow travellers on their long path up the sacred mountain. This was greeted with some trademark Miller mirth, and was clearly also well wide of the mark. Hamish is quite categorical that the reason he came back from the other side, was that he chose to do so - because he felt so inadequate. There was so much more he needed to learn, or at least to absorb, before he was ready to make even the smallest contribution to the seismic scenario in the sky.

Once back on the same plane as the rest of us, Hamish's outlook, his attitude and his whole raison d'être had changed. His vision, his horizons and his perspectives were irrevocably widened. Once you have seen the boundless vistas of the Promised Land, a trip to the fish and chip shop, even on a day when there's a two-for-the-price-of-one offer on the pickled eggs, will never seem quite so exciting again.

> When I look back now to the time before the NDE, I feel it was a completely useless life, even with the Jaguar and all the paraphernalia that goes with the world of business. It was such a very, very narrow field. While you are in it, it's the be-all and end-all of your life. I had been making quite a bit of money and that had been very satisfying in some ways, but it was a way of life that had very narrow parameters - and I knew there had to be something outside them. So, I moved to Cornwall to try to reconcile these strange feelings that something was going to happen. I had no idea what it was likely to be. I was aware that I was now open to a whole raft of ideas and activities that I hadn't even known about before the NDE.

As it turned out, one of the avenues that opened up was an introduction to the arcane art of dowsing.

The search for the subtle serpent

To make sense of the next part of this book, you will need a rudimentary introduction to dowsing. You don't need to be able to dowse, although there's a good chance that you can - whoever you are and wherever or whenever you are reading this paragraph. Indeed, I can say, with some conviction, that you are already a latent dowser.

What is dowsing?

In its simplest form, dowsing is just the sensing of those things that are not evidently detectable by the five gross senses. What has traditionally tended to separate dowsing from general sixth senseness and universal clairvoyance is the use of dowsing tools - bent metal rods of an appropriate size, a pendulum, a Y-shaped hazel twig or indeed anything that can give you a visible indication of the answer to the question you have asked.

Hamish dowsing at Launceston Castle using his own hand-forged rods

There is nothing very special about the chosen dowsing tool of preference. You just have to be comfortable handling it and to be able to understand what it is telling you.

Dowsing is also a process; a deliberate attempt to get information that would generally be regarded as unobtainable from traditional sources. Whilst dowsing results can often be checked and cross-referenced by examining the written record or by digging a hole in the ground, the importance of them is that they are the direct result of asking questions with definitive yes/no answers.

Almost everyone can dowse to some extent. It's a bit like riding a bike or learning to swim. Most people can do it. Some don't want to do it for various reasons and some have a mental block about doing it, but they tend to be a small minority. If you want to give it a try, and I strongly recommend that you do, just get yourself on one of the weekend courses run by an accredited tutor of the British Society of Dowsers. It will use up very little of this life cycle, not cost a fortune and will activate, one might even say liberate, a skill that men and women have used since time immemorial. For some, it remains a fascinating sideline (although it is no party trick), but for others it is a Eureka moment, when you realise that there really is something out there - and you can prove it to yourself.

As with any skill, there are two factors that effectively determine whether, like Hamish, it becomes a way of life and a way of earning a living or, like me, you can be competent enough to know that it is a real phenomenon, but you wouldn't class yourself as an expert. The two factors are innate ability, which you will have to a greater or lesser degree - and practice, practice, practice.

Most people come to dowsing with a healthy, sometimes outspoken, scepticism. That's an excellent starting place. But most of those who take the time to come to at least one training session also have a second important attribute - an open mind. The post-NDE Hamish Miller certainly had a fair dollop of both.

What use is dowsing?

On one level, the use to which dowsing can be put is only restricted by your imagination. Consequently, those like Hamish, who have had that facility externally expanded have a head start.

In practical terms, dowsing is generally used for:

- Locating hidden and/or underground water, electricity and telephone cables, gas and water pipes, mineral deposits, tunnels, mineshafts . . .

- Archaeological investigation, such as finding lost buildings, the location of previous features such as wells, hearths and sacred sites, buried stone rows, fallen menhirs, ploughed up tumuli and fortifications . . .

- Healing - non-invasive, usually hands on or energy work at a distance, diagnosing energy imbalances (where there is a considerable overlap with acupuncture and other oriental medical practices), seeking appropriate herbal and non-pharmaceutical remedies . . .

- Earth energy investigation, including the geological energy networks, planetary grids, ley lines, the impact and rebalancing of natural and man-generated detrimental energies . . .

- Finding the answer to just about any question that you can frame clearly - and to keep in mind in sufficient concentration, to enable you to produce a yes/no answer using your rods, or a pendulum or whatever device you choose to use. In this mode, the mind seems to operate a bit like a computer without the wires - well, without the chips. Somewhere 'out there' seems to be an information field, where every piece of knowledge is stored and, under certain circumstances, everyone can access it, with enough practice and a sound intent. This then starts to overlap with parallel, cutting-edge thinking in sub-atomic physics . . .

. . . and that's just some of the main chapter headings.

One classic use of dowsing is in finding your way when you are lost. My wife, Ros, and I had been invited to the launch of Hamish's *Definitive Wee Book of Dowsing*. However, the launch fell on a day when I had already organised a Tamar Dowsers event, so sadly we put the invite behind the clock and assumed we wouldn't be going. When the day arrived, Cornwall was suffering from extreme winds and driving rain and the dowsing event had to be called off at the last minute. Ros remembered the book launch, and after a short discussion around 'Is your journey really necessary?' we decided to go anyway. Little did we know just how badly West Cornwall had been affected. As we turned off the main road towards St Ives, the route to Hamish's house was blocked by fallen trees and we had to back up with some difficulty, only to be diverted to . . . well, to this day, I'm not entirely sure where. All I know

is that we were about as far from anywhere recognisable on a map as you can get in Penwith - and in low cloud and fading light we hadn't the slightest idea of how to track back to our intended destination.
Eventually, we ended up at a sign-free T-junction and just looked at each other. In the absence of rational deduction, there was only one thing for it - out came the rods. I asked if I should go left and got a clear 'yes'. A little later on, we hit a fork in the road, so out came the rods again. Each time we had to choose, I asked a straight 'yes/no' question and got a straight response. Half an hour later, we rolled into Hamish's drive from an unexpected direction. Dowsing for directions to the launch of a book about dowsing seemed a very relevant use of the skill.

Earthly energetics

What is generally termed Earth Energy is actually a worldwide lattice of winding, or serpentine, lines of force which appear to emanate from the earth itself. They are very likely to be geological in nature, or at least closely geologically related. As you will see later, these lines have individual characteristics. What seems to the novice dowser to be a single unit, a single piece of rope, an experienced diviner can disentangle into a myriad of strands, each responding to their own colour. The resultant sense is of an invisible, but intricate, technicolour tapestry in the ground.

After water, Earth Energy is usually the easiest to locate for the beginner - and there are few people who cannot sense it using the crudest of dowsing tools within a few minutes, once they have got the hang of what to do.

Earth Energy seems to have been a top priority on the agenda of ancient man, given the high profile it is given at sacred spaces and important places all over the world.

In recent years, however, a new dimension in the study of Earth Energy has evolved with the realisation that objects of considerable mass, perhaps aided by certain types of crystalline composition, actually attract earth energy lines to them. There are numerous before-and-after studies that show how the placing of a large stone, or Menhir, will cause a line to move from some distance away to rest under the stone. The work of the Northern Ireland dowser, Billy Gawn, is seminal in the understanding of this process.

This throws into question whether sacred sites were located to mark or to attract such energy, but suffice to say for the time being, that the two clearly have some kind of symbiotic relationship.

The development of dowsing

Having been made illegal under the Witchcraft Act of 1562, during the reign of Elizabeth I, and only partially decriminalised in 1951 (just in time for me to make an appearance in this cycle) dowsing is still a very young discipline and it is evolving all the time. Even in the twenty years or so that I have been involved with it, huge strides have been made in the understanding of the technique.

Increasingly, the more sensitive and talented dowsers are 'going deviceless', eschewing the rods for the tingling of fingertips or even just training the muscles of their eyes. Journeymen practitioners like myself are only too keen to use this advanced technique when we need to, but usually we still seek the reassurance of the rods for confirmation. The parallel with riding a bike using stabilisers, or swimming with a rubber ring, seems very apt in this context.

Dowsing survived for 400 years as (almost literally) an underground art mainly due to the activities of the revered water diviner, who in rural areas performed a vital local service to farmers and country folk. Today, it is felt that some of the procedures adopted by the wild-eyed old diviner, waving a large hazel branch around to find the best site for a well, owed as much to protective theatre and feigned madness than to actual need. It is likely that, at a time when there was less in the way of electromagnetic interference, lower noise levels and fewer other distractions, most experienced diviners could probably have virtually walked to the right place and stuck a pole in the selected spot ready to start digging - but they would then have risked being burnt at the stake for their troubles.

So why don't we use dowsing all the time?

The first answer is an historical one. Queen Elizabeth's ban may not have killed off dowsing completely - after all it's a bit like trying to ban listening - but it did cut off the tradition from its roots. If road-building was prevented for a few centuries, eventually someone would rediscover it or re-import it, and the skill would become re-established in a different social environment, but probably using different materials and different technology.

The second, and perhaps most important reason, is credibility. We live in a world that has had a material, scientific base since that interestingly termed period, The Enlightenment. Towards the end of the 17th century, much of the hogwash and superstition that had plagued earlier cultures was flushed down the drain - but with it went a vast heritage of researching real phenomena that were associated with the discredited worldview. A phrase about babies and bathwater comes to mind. In the case of dowsing, out went baby, bathwater, soap dish, plumbing and water treatment plant.

The organised western religions survived the firestorm with a very modern business model. Clear objectives, good PR and effective marketing, use of the legal system to protect existing patents, a mountainous bankroll, excellent networking with the movers and shakers . . . Dowsers and healers, shamen and wise women, were always marginal figures and, worse still, they were outsiders with influence and information that could not easily be suppressed by dictat - dangerous folk, loose cannons to have about in a lifestyle that was sharpening at the edges.

Dowsing became associated with the old order, the pre-scientific world, and was therefore disregarded, ridiculed, and actively suppressed.

From the perspective of the 21st century, this may seem an odd conclusion for the emerging scientific world to reach. After all, the impressive breakthroughs of science have been very much at the expense of the remaindered deity. Most of the attributes previously bestowed on the spiritual source have been incrementally explained - at least to the satisfaction of the general public. The weather, the movements of the planets, dysfunctional physical health, forces like electricity, gravity and radiation have all been systematically investigated and described in a way that most people can understand. Dowsing, and its associated phenomena, remains at the cutting edge of discovery.

One can argue that non-physical sciences such as psychology, took a long time to come in out of the cold, and even then only on the basis that there must be some physical basis to them, in the Newtonian sense of the word.

However, just as there was electricity before Faraday and gravity before Newton, the sense, or medium, or force, or force-field that provides the platform for dowsing is awaiting a flash, young, post-scientific whiz-kid to give it an acceptable media persona.

The British Society of Dowsers

Today, dowsing in the UK is promoted and co-ordinated by The British
Society of Dowsers (BSD). Formed in 1933 (some 18 years before
dowsing was decriminalised, you will note!), the BSD exists to encourage
the study and enhance the knowledge of the subject in all its forms,
amongst both members and the general public.

In the early years, the BSD was run largely by former senior military
personnel and retired academics - respectable and respected people, many
of whom had been trained to dowse on military operations, found that it
worked for them and had a serious scientific interest in both explaining
and using the phenomenon. In the period before the cultural revolution of
the 1960s, doubtless this narrow cross-section of society would have been
the only proponents of the skill who would have been taken seriously in
the wider world. However, certainly since the turn of the millennium, the
BSD has become a broad-based community, with a growing international
component, populated in part by practising professional dowsers, like
Hamish, and augmented by lay members, like myself, who enjoy and
appreciate dowsing, but who have a day-job in another, albeit rather more
mundane, world.

Membership of the Society is open to anyone interested in dowsing,
regardless of ability. A comprehensive training curriculum is provided
that can take the complete beginner right through to advanced practitioner
level.

Apart from maintaining a small dedicated team at their office in a
converted farm building in Worcestershire, the BSD has local groups all
across the UK, run by volunteers, each with their own local interests and
activities.

There are also a number of national BSD Special Interest Groups which
meet periodically to discuss, and practise the use of dowsing in specific
realms of activity - these include archaeology, health, earth energy and
water.

Hamish was an active member of the BSD for 27 years and was very
supportive of the organisation:

> The BSD does a lot of excellent work in encouraging the use
> of the skill - and in providing a framework for the
> development and protection of dowsers.

There are still plenty of people who are keen to disparage the whole idea of using your intuition to help you understand the world around you - both from a scientific and a religious perspective. The BSD is very valuable in supporting the individual dowser in this respect.

I have attended many BSD events, and spoken at some of them. The benefit you can gain from getting together with other dowsers, many of whom have totally different approaches to the subject from yourself, cannot be overstated.

The greatest pleasure of the BSD events is that you get to spend time with like-minded people in a relaxed atmosphere. Quite frankly, if nothing useful happened at these workshops at all, it would still be great fun just to be there.

Given the profound nature of what dowsing can enable the experienced user to discover, the BSD has to have a very clear code of ethics, to which all members (including Hamish and myself) agree to adhere. This is detailed at Appendix A.

If you become interested in having a go at dowsing as a result of reading this book, contact details for the BSD are also included in that Appendix.

There are also a growing number of sister organisations across the world, which pursue similar types of agenda, but naturally with their own national and regional characteristics.

The future of dowsing

There are many in the dowsing community who would like to see dowsing become a fully-fledged scientific discipline in its own right. But dowsing totters at the edge of respectability for one very good reason - the ability to provide reliable replication in a laboratory environment.

There are plenty of studies that have provided a solid evidence base for the verification of a genuine phenomenon. Lynn McTaggart's *The Field* is an illustrative work in this area. However, dowsing is so subtle, so transient, so close to the edge of nothingness that it can't easily be unpackaged by the technician.

In my experience, a good dowser, in a quiet and meditative state, away from distraction and on a site that is either conducive to deep concentration, or at least neutral from interference by EMFs, can get the 'right answer' to most clear questions 70% - 80% of the time. This is way, way above any level of chance. It would convince me, even if I couldn't actually sense anything myself, that we are dealing with something real - in the planet earth sense of the word. There are some dowsers, particularly experienced water diviners who are tapping into a much deeper tradition, who can well exceed that. Those who work on a 'no water, no fee' basis need a hit rate of over 90% to remain solvent. The legendary Cornish diviner, Donovan Wilkins, fell firmly into this group. Even the most sceptical statistician would have trouble explaining away that sort of accuracy. Put those same people in the lab and the results are very different - their hit rate still way above the statistically significant, but it is not regularly repeatable and therefore not scientifically sound, as such.

As we shall see later, even the great Hamish Miller looked pretty ordinary, working to an artificial deadline on an early episode of Channel 4's Time Team. The archaeologists dug where he had marked the spot and . . . nothing was found. Dowsing failed to reappear on the programme.

There are those who are happy with it that way. If the scientific basis of dowsing were to be discovered and vivisected, it would then be available to those with a variety of motives - the weaver of spells and the voodoo worker, the arms manufacturer and the merchant banker. I was taught that dowsing doesn't work if you seek to use it for personal gain, such as lottery numbers, nor for negative purposes, but the jury is still out.

Dowsing evangelists see it as a potentially scientifically spiritualising force (if that's not too much of a contradiction in terms), which would inject enlightenment into the veins of a species that seems to be hell-bent on heading for oblivion up the cul-de-sac of monetary materialism. However, the new 'old school' would prefer to retain it as a valuable tool for quietly offsetting the madness of the majority. Perhaps as a reaction to the tendency of postmodern societies to deconstruct both maladies and remedies alike, they would counsel against delving too deeply into why it actually works.

Hamish clearly had a foot in both camps, but took a characteristically independent view of the skill.

> It's very hard to prove to the satisfaction of the scientific community. If I could invent a dowsing rod with a gauge and little numbers on it, I am sure more people would believe it.

The discoveries of Alfred Nobel with respect to the energy potential of the atom are an interesting comparative study. Nobel thought he was unveiling a practical, free and unlimited form of energy, which would release mankind from the limitations of the previous technological era and provide vast amounts of time and opportunity to investigate the higher elements of human endeavour. Along with it came Hiroshima and Nagasaki, Chernobyl and Three Mile Island - and considerable amounts of irradiated spent fuel, with a half-life longer than anyone alive today, that we still haven't the slightest idea what to do with on a permanent basis. While all information is inherently neutral, the people who inherit it, and the society into which it falls, are anything but.

Yet, like the apparition you catch sight of at the corner of your vision, the more you try to bring dowsing into sharper focus, the more you try to pick it apart, the more it seems to fade from your gaze. We are certainly dealing with a dimension that we do not fully comprehend and one which seems intent (and I use the word deliberately) on not disclosing itself to us - at least not yet.

Learning to dowse

There are good, down-to-earth dowsing tutors working quietly all over the UK. A register of approved instructors is kept by the British Society of Dowsers and can be accessed via their website. Alternatively, just tap in 'dowsing' and where you live and I'd be surprised if you didn't come up with a local dowser or dowsing group to talk to.

It's not difficult and it's not spooky - unless you're very easily spooked - but it could be a weekend that changes your life. Give it a try and come to your own conclusions.

While I was taught by Alan Neal, and inspired by Hamish and by Billy Gawn, HM himself was largely self-taught and he had little formal tuition. He made his own trademark rods in his own forge and he selected his own fields of research. After the NDE, he became firmly convinced that he was being subtly led in the direction of personal discovery and development. If he was to become even the errand-boy of The Management, he had to get to grips with at least the basics of the non-physical world. He openly acknowledged the importance and influence of books that he subsequently read by John Michell, Tom Graves and Sig Lonegren, to name but a few, but that information only came after he was already an established dowser.

As we have seen in previous chapters, Hamish was a self-starter, who ploughed his own furrow. He listened to others and accepted their help - but it was one of his basic principles that you should work it out for yourself; prove it (or refute it) for yourself. Hamish was a prime exponent of the view that dowsing is a do-it-yourself activity, a feel-it-for-yourself experience.

HM taught dowsing himself to all and sundry and ran his inimitable training days for several decades. Often these were held at Treviscoe, his home near Hayle in Cornwall. He felt strongly that it was one of his most worthwhile ventures in the field.

> I love teaching at dowsing workshops. I love seeing people's faces when they start dowsing for the first time. It's so rewarding. I wish I could have photographed the expressions on the faces of all those people. Ba and I have been doing it for years. There's no stress, it's just a pure pleasure.

> It's actually spreading the word about dowsing, which I think is so important. It's my way; it's not the only way, but it's certainly a practical way, to show that there is something beyond the five senses. That's the message I'm trying to give out, because having had these experiences of near-death and of enlightenment through dowsing, you become very sure of what is to come after the end of this cycle.

A New Path up the Mountain

I have always been attracted to a very wise quotation, attributed to the Buddha, that (words to the effect that) there are as many ways up the mountain as there are people in the world - but there is still only one mountain.

On meeting Michael

By 1983, Hamish no longer saw his original path of engineering entrepreneurship as sufficiently rewarding. He was being drawn, by a confluence of circumstances, towards a new way of working with the world he now found himself inhabiting. This environment was, to put it mildly, unknown territory.

Part of that new path was leading him up the winding way of the diviner.

> When I came down to Cornwall, I was recuperating. A big influence on me at the time was a clairvoyant called Michael Colmer, who came round to see my late wife, because she had asked him for a reading. When he first visited my house, Jean was out shopping. I invited him in and he looked at me and said 'Who are you, and what are you doing?' I told him, and he asked 'Are you into healing?' I'd never heard of it, so I asked 'Why?' He replied with 'Well you should be, because you've got a big blue aura'. I thought 'I've got a right nutter here'. I hadn't been into that sort of thing at all.

Michael Colmer

Then he started talking about other things, like earth energy. He took me up to the top of Trencrom Hill, where he introduced me to an 'Earth Energy Centre'. He said 'This is where the centre is and it can have a profound effect on your life'. I thought he was talking absolute nonsense. He said 'You're not only going to heal people, you'll be healing the earth'. That didn't mean anything to me either. I thought this man was right out of his tiny mind, so I hastened to get rid of him. Just as I was ushering him round the corner, he said, 'You know, in about six months time, you'll be giving a lecture about this'. I said 'Michael, you are stark staring, raving mad. I don't know anything about this stuff and I certainly couldn't give a talk on it. Anyway, I've never given a talk in my life and I'm not going to start now. It's been nice to see you, goodbye!'

As it turned out, Michael was spot on with his timing.

On meeting Colin

Despite his protestations, Hamish was soon to find out a great deal about 'this stuff', but maybe not quite in the way he might have expected.

Shortly after meeting Michael Colmer, I saw a notice in the paper that Colin Bloy was giving a lecture on dowsing and healing in Devon. Colin was quite well known in alternative circles at the time, because he had started Fountain International near where I used to live in Sussex. I decided to go along. Fountain International was a group, based in Brighton, which gathered like-minded people together to heal places, rather than people. It started in response to the annual problems in the summer when large gangs of Mods and Rockers came down from London to terrorise the locals and generally cause mayhem (or an imbalance of energy as we call it in the trade).

I was very impressed with Colin. He was a good speaker: his timing was exceptional; he was witty and very, very well informed. Sadly, he's dead now, but he was great. I was absolutely on a high when he'd finished, so I approached him after the talk and asked if he could point me in the direction of a local dowser, because I wanted to work with standing stones near my home down in Cornwall. He looked at me and said 'Do it yourself' and walked away. I was shattered, because I thought he had just slammed the door shut in my face - but of course, like the riddles of a Buddhist guru, he'd said precisely the right thing.

Hamish with Colin Bloy

Six months later, I went down to my forge and I thought 'Sod Colin Bloy - I <u>will</u> do this'. I hammered out a big dowsing rod, wandered up the road a bit and found the first wavering earth energy line between St Michael's Mount and Trencrom Hill. That moment profoundly changed my life.

Through my work with Colin, I met Roger Brown, an Australian, and we worked together one weekend looking at energy lines in Sussex, which were very like the ones I had found at Trencrom.

Out of the blue, he asked me 'What colour are they?' I couldn't grasp what he was talking about, so he elaborated 'Well, this one responds to the question 'Is this a yellow line, and that one to blue, and that to the question is this a green one'. I thought he'd lost the plot, but it was just Mother Earth explaining to a peasant like myself that they were different frequencies, and they responded to different questions about the colours of lines. It took me quite a while to take in the implications.

Expanding the horizons

When I came back to Cornwall, I started to work out what the various frequencies of the lines were. I found that they dowsed like a mirror image as you walked across the line. If you had a line that responded to red on the outside, you'd get red, yellow, blue - not necessarily the sequence of a rainbow, but you would get different colours. When you got to the centre, they would be in the reverse order going out to the red one on the outside, which was kind of strange.

I just noted it. It was part of a completely innocent investigation of all these strange things that were becoming available to me through dowsing.

I found later that the centre line changed and stopped responding to my concept of colours, although it did respond for a time to the sense of gold and silver. I couldn't think of anything else beyond that, and I felt stuck. I had a range of colour that I was conscious of, but there were two lines in the centre of the band that didn't respond to any of them.

I remember going through masses of different ideas and concepts without success, until I got to Ancient Knowledge. I got an immediate response on Ancient Knowledge - at least to my perception of Ancient Knowledge. I thought, 'I've cracked it. I've cracked it. I can get into the Akashic Records (which we will talk about in more detail later).' I sat down with great ceremony in the middle of this line in the garden and, very po-faced, exclaimed 'I am ready' - but this great voice in my head replied 'No, you're not' which rather cut me down to size. I can laugh about it now, but I was devastated at the time. I thought I was just on the verge of some monumental discovery - but I wasn't really, I wasn't even asking the right questions.

Once I got going, certain lines responded to my questions about the association with love, hate, anger and various other emotions. I obviously had a problem with the language I was using, because I wasn't getting the sort of positive responses I expected. Sometimes, I would just get a flicker from the rods, which I came to realise meant that I hadn't got my words right. However, gradually I began to understand more of the detail of the complex composition of the lines. The line in the garden began to have a characteristic feel. It had, at that time, maybe 20 different bands of energy, but it started to expand. The next week I would work with it, and it had grown to 40 or more. I thought it was because these frequencies were already there, and I was getting a little more sensitive as I gained experience. In due course, I came to realise that it was actually responding to the fact that I was working with it. But the implication behind that was so immense, that I didn't want to believe it.

About 18 months or so went by, just experimenting, going out at different times of the day, finding that the energy moved, and the bands moved. Sometimes they would line up in one direction in the morning, but they could change direction during the day, and then they would be different again in the evening. I began to realise that the whole earth energy matrix was dynamic, and it was changing in real time. It was an incredibly exciting, completely unexpected, natural function and I felt it was so important that we should find out about it. It was very tangibly there; I wasn't imagining it - all the same, I felt I had to get other dowsers to check my findings.

Roger Brown had done something similar in Australia, and Colin was already way in advance of what I was finding. He was dowsing with his hands - deviceless as we call it nowadays - and he was starting to dowse incredible shapes in the ground. I didn't get into that until I worked with him again in Brighton. He found some manifestations, which were gradually changing shape over time, sometimes over six months, sometimes in shorter periods.

Working with energy grids

We started working with the Fountain Grid. This was the first of the energy grids I had experienced. It was, and still is, a rectilinear mesh that can be dowsed on the ground, which reacts to natural phenomena and to the intervention of the dowser. Colin Bloy introduced me to the whole concept of the earth having energy. He just seemed to come across it, but it's part of a whole complex multi-dimensional matrix of subtle forces.

I think he became aware of the grid, because of his feeling that he could give healing to places by applying healing to the 'hara', the energy centre. His method was to find the energy centre of the area he was trying to balance and then to apply a conscious acknowledgement of it - or as he said, just give it love. Colin had the theory that if we could heal the earth, people would also be healed by the fact that the earth around them was healed and that it wasn't threatening them. He felt that if every village could have a 'hara' and you could put energy into it, then the energy would reach out - and maybe go all round the world. Ironically, that's just what we do have, a 'hara' in every village, but most of them are tucked away inside big stone buildings! If we could liberate these 'church-haras' from the baggage of the past millennium, we might really be on to something that could set the world on to a very different course.

Colin picked up a reaction from the earth, from his acknowledgement that it was alive and moving dynamically. He interpreted it as a huge grid, consisting of a mesh of squares each of about 100 metres by 100 metres. Gradually, as you worked with it, it closed up progressively, until it became such a fine mesh that it was almost impossible to dowse at all.

Today, dowsers work a lot with other energy grids, of which the Hartmann Grid and the Curry Grid are the best known. The Hartmann tends to be dowsed as a series of vertical and horizontal lines - a bit like the way latitude and longitude is indicated on a globe, but with a much finer mesh. The Curry is a similar type of mesh, but is offset at an angle, so that you end up dowsing diamond shapes, rather than oblongs. These are just two of the simpler formats of earth energy.

Earth energy structures are infinitely variable, and I can find no rigid rules to define them. I take up cudgels with a lot of people in the dowsing world, because I have checked on a dozen people's interpretations and they all tend to differ in detail. Some people claim that a grid is, say, 2.6 metres by 1.8 metres, and that's it - fact. To me, that's an absolute nonsense, because there is nothing static about the whole earth energy network. It varies in size depending on all sorts of things that we don't understand yet. It's part of the complexity of the three, or four, dimensional matrix.

**Fountain Grid marked out on the lawn
at Treviscoe by Hamish**

When I came back to Cornwall, I tried to make some sense of Colin's discoveries concerning the Fountain Grid that he had passed on to me. I soon found that simple interpretations were not sophisticated enough to explain all the various components that I was starting to find. The first step was to locate the Fountain Grid on a flat space that I could work with, so I found a workable part of it on the lawn and I started to mark it out - with drain clearing rods. I marked out the squares there and photographed them.

I found that there were significant variations in the form and the size of the grid at different times of the day and, as you worked with it, it would get smaller and smaller. Given the climate down here, I decided to replicate the process inside, on the floor of the cottage. It started out as a sort of 15-inch square grid, but as I worked with it, it reduced in size, until it was tiny. Ultimately, in two places, the lines were so close together, that I could hardly measure the distance between them at all. In another place, I found a crossing point of the two bunched sets of grid lines. As I worked with them, the gridlines started to close up together, until they formed bands that were almost solid. It was fascinating, but very difficult to get your head around.

The new received wisdom on the subject of these energy highways is that they form part of a global energy network. They seem to derive either from the underlying geology of the earth or, perhaps more likely, from the effect of the planet spinning through space. Either way, they are natural organic manifestations with effects that can be sensed and considered by anyone with an enquiring mind and a bent coat hanger.

Having established that there is a general consensus that grids of various types do exist, perhaps the more important implication is that this extremely low level energy is being pumped and circulated around the world and is therefore available for use.

People from various cultures with differing attitudes to such energy appear to have become aware of this circulating energy and to have reacted to it in a way that was largely dictated by their own upbringing and previous experience. It seems that they all felt the need to mark the grids, or at least the grid crossing points where the energy was most in evidence, in some significant way.

> To be honest, I'm rather uncomfortable about the way grid systems are being portrayed in dowsing circles. You tend to get people presenting neat little diagrams of how the energy goes round the world, and it's usually a geodetic structure and I don't think the world is like that. As I've said before, I don't believe that the Hartmann grid is a specific size and I don't believe that the Curry grid is a specific size.

> The implication behind these theories is that the earth is a rigid structure, a crystalline structure, which doesn't budge, which has no feelings, which has no energy of its own. In a Druidic tradition, which as far as I understand, was not written down, the Earth has twelve major circular lines going around it. Where these encircling lines intersect are very important and sacred places.

> With regard to these major grid lines, I think that parts of two of the circles have a major crossing point at St Michael's Mount. I think that's seriously important, because two pairs of powerful lines cross there, an occurrence that is found at very few other places around the world.

> However, there are doubtless other sites that do host such invisible junctions and consequently exhibit strong and complex positive energy. Jerusalem, Lhasa and Uluru are obvious nodal points - and possibly Damanhur in northern Italy, which looks really interesting.

> That's one place I'd like to check out before I get the call to
> beetle back up the tunnel.

For Hamish, there was always going to be unfinished business.

The radiance of radials

It's not just the planetary-scale earth energy grids that brought Hamish to
an understanding of the interconnectivity of all things. He had been
aware from his earliest ventures into the field of dowsing that each entity
- animal, vegetable or mineral - exhibited a number of dowsable, straight
lines leading out from it. The former cyclist described these as radials, as
in the spokes of a wheel. The more massive or more energetic the object,
the stronger or more numerous the radials.

He found that these spokes were not just hypothetical lines in a
hermetically sealed void, but were potentially linked spears of force.
Each line reached out towards the radials of other entities. Where they
established a common energy continuum, a line of attraction would bind
the objects together invisibly. Places, stones, trees, people - all seemed to
be holding hands ethereally across the landscape. He came to appreciate
that in a very real and demonstrable sense we are effectively all as one
with each other - and all as one with the world around us.

Certain spiritual luminaries have voiced such ideas across the ages, but
for most of us these ideas were too ephemeral to have any real meaning.
Yet here was an 'ordinary bloke' demonstrating this profound principle in
a way that we didn't just have to take on trust or for granted. We could
check out for ourselves with any bit of wire or stick from the hedge. It
was a quietly dramatic breakthrough.

> To me, it's a part of the earth's nervous system. I describe
> the links as radials, but effectively they're just like little
> neuropeptides, quietly pulsing away to themselves like
> they've been doing for the last 60 million years, or whatever.
> Their manifestation to me, and to hundreds of other dowsers,
> is that each neuropeptide is putting out a number of
> connections to its neighbours, as a part of a matrix. It's
> sitting within its own energy spiral and suddenly an external
> consciousness logs a message in.

This is a very similar process to what happens with ourselves. We get a conscious, or an unconscious, message that comes into one of our neuropeptides - and the neuropeptide seems to decide whether to forward this information on, or not. There is quite a debate going on at the moment as to whether they have 'intelligence', as all the indications are that they can block the onward transmission of the message if they choose to do so.

**Radials marked out by Hamish on the carpet
at the energy centre at Treviscoe**

To me, an earth energy centre is a neuropeptide of the earth. This is why, when you start dowsing it, it reacts and sends out more radials to other places, passing on the information to other energy centres that you are actively participating.

As we will see later, he found that the radial network is not an inert thing 'out there', but it is a living entity that develops in response to the input of the observer - and to the interest of the dowser.

Eclipsed by the value of dowsing

I was dowsing every evening, just to check what had happened to the Fountain Grid. Then, one evening, I found I couldn't get a reaction at all. I was shattered when I found I couldn't dowse the energy - it was like losing a leg. If I couldn't dowse any more, then I would have been a partially lost soul. I felt I was just at the beginning of finding out about something incredibly important, and I was absolutely devastated.

I went outside, just to get a breath of fresh air, and wondered to myself what the hell had gone wrong. By chance, I looked up - and there was a partial eclipse of the moon, which had patently affected the whole energy matrix. I went back in again and started to dowse. The grid had gone, but my little indoor energy centre had acquired straight radial lines fanning out from a single point. I walked round and counted 14 of them. They were not evenly spaced, for reasons that I found out later.

That was the beginning of a huge voyage of discovery about what happens with earth energy. The relief that came, when I realised that I could still dowse, flooded all over me. It was almost overwhelming. I can't tell you how completely bereft I was when I found I'd lost the art. I thought to myself, 'How can you live without dowsing, once you know what it can do?'

The experience with the eclipse started a whole series of experiments. I worked with this little energy centre, and found that sometimes there were 14 radials, sometimes there were 16, sometimes there were 18, but it always reverted to the basic 14 at rest.

Another highly significant discovery; another 'hair rising on the back of the neck' event occurred when I felt prompted to "see if there are any other manifestations". I chose one of the radials over by the corner, and I walked along it. The rod turned about six times, and I just marked the points on the floor with drawing pins. I chose another radial, and it did the same thing. Finally I went round them all, and put the drawing pins in the floor. I stood back, but it just didn't mean anything at all. It was a bitter disappointment, because I felt there was something specific happening there. I walked over and stood over the top of it, and I was almost in tears because I realised that the drawing pins were in an absolutely perfect Fibonacci spiral.

The Fibonacci 'spiral' is in fact a series of linked quarter-circles,

Nautilus shell

connected arithmetically by a factor known as the Golden Mean. It's easier to show than to explain. It's quite common in nature - the marine creature, the Nautilus, has a shell shape that is often cited as a perfect example of a Fibonacci spiral.

However, the plot thickens when the Fibonacci pattern pops up not just in the spiral formation of sunflower seed heads or the bark of palm trees, but also in exploding galaxies, gothic cathedrals and even crop circles - but more of this later.

As a blacksmith, I make spirals in metal, but I couldn't have contrived anything anywhere near as perfect as that. You can't mark 40 different points and expect them to be in the right position, unless you're actually measuring something real. It was just an absolutely perfect spiral. I didn't know a lot about Fibonacci spirals then, but afterwards I looked into the business of the number of plants and natural things that are composed of them … snails, cones, flowers. The Fibonacci spiral is a fundamental building block of life itself - and I had been shown it in my own front room!

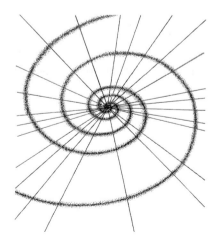

Fibonacci spiral at the Treviscoe energy centre

For months, I carried out experiments with the spiral - and it kept playing with me. I got the sensation that The Management were leading me through a process, so that I would get a deeper understanding of what was happening. The spiral started to change formation. It would wind up under certain conditions, and manifest eight turns between the end of the fireplace and the centre of the spiral. Then it would wind down to six or even four turns.

There were so many different factors affecting it that I couldn't tell exactly what was doing what. I discovered later that sometimes there was a second little spiral starting from the inside, and then a third. Something or somebody seemed to be playing with me - or rather, I was being fed information at the sort of rate that I would be able to absorb, and possibly, later on, I might begin to understand what it was all about.

There is little doubt, looking at it with the benefit of hindsight, that the NDE had opened up Hamish's heart and his consciousness to new opportunities. This, in turn, presented the possibility of a meeting with Colin and, perhaps rather more pertinently, of Hamish feeling that Colin's ideas were worth further consideration. A pre-1982 HM would have dismissed them as so much mumbo-jumbo - in fact, he may not even have registered them at all.

Once on the New Path, the focused Scot was on the case, but with renewed vigour and a much broader outlook. He might have felt he was on to something big, but even he had no concept of just how BIG it would turn out to be.

Hamish Miller's World of Dowsing

A few months after the strange encounter with Michael Colmer, mentioned earlier, Hamish was indeed asked to give a talk about dowsing.

Michael Colmer said, when he left my house that I would soon be doing talks about dowsing - and I disagreed. However, barely six weeks after I had joined the National Federation of Healers, the lady from the local NFH branch called me on the phone. She said that they were very short of money - and she asked me if I would do a talk about dowsing for them, to raise a bit of income. I heard myself say 'Of course, I'll do a talk about dowsing' - and then I thought 'Michael Colmer, you bastard!'

On the appointed evening, I went up to St Mabyn Village Hall to do the talk, but I was absolutely terrified. The organiser of the NFH group, Sheila Jeffries, asked me to arrive at seven o'clock, so that we could prepare for the meeting, which was due to start at half past seven. It was a really black November night across the moors, and the event was to be held in a little hut that was locked up when we arrived. At 7.15, I said to her 'I think we'll just go to the pub' - we hadn't even got the keys. However, she wasn't to be put off and she soon found the keyholder. She opened the door and we put out half a dozen chairs - but by 7.29 there still wasn't anybody there. Again, I said that I thought we should just pack up and go home. It was my first talk and I really didn't want to do it. She asked me to wait a few more minutes - and at that moment the door burst open and about 30 people came in from the pub next door - including Paul Broadhurst, with whom I later collaborated for several years. I can't remember anything about the talk at all, but at the end of it there were 15 pairs of people walking round the room with bent-wire dowsing rods. The next thing I knew, the verger was beating at the door, saying 'You've got to get out'. It was 9.30, and I was in the business of teaching people how to dowse.

From Cornwall to Norfolk

There have been many other dowsers and many other people who have described, quite adequately, both the phenomenon and the use to which it can be put in the everyday world. If the peak of the Miller mastery had been that he had learned to dowse, this would have been a rather short book and arguably there would have been little reason to write this book at all. The big difference between Hamish and the rest of us, some of whom may have become half-decent dowsers, is the way he has taken the skill beyond the sphere of the worthy and practical and into the domain of the profound and the philosophical.

Shortly after the meetings with Colin and Michael, Hamish met and became friends with the late John Michell. John had been writing books at the cutting edge of emerging creativity and credibility for a couple of decades. I still have two of them on my bookshelf that date from the mid-1970s. While I found them an oblique, even obscure, take on the unexplained mysteries of the time, Hamish realised that John was on to something significant and that he, Hamish, might be able to take it forward.

One of John's visionary revelations, perhaps in turn following in the footsteps of Alfred Watkins, was to have stood on Glastonbury Tor and seen, or sensed, a line of energy reaching out to the western horizon and beyond, passing through St Michael's Mount. Exactly what he felt and how he felt it we cannot be sure for certain, but he was sufficiently convincing in his description of this strange phenomenon to inspire the newly-dowsing HM to investigate it.

Back in West Cornwall, Hamish started to look for John's line. Eventually he found what seemed to be the right energy and set about trying to trace it in the local vicinity. Understandably, given Watkins's theory and Michell's description, Hamish started to look for a straight alignment. It seemed a fascinating, and fairly simple idea - find the appropriate energy line and trace it across the country, at least as far as Glastonbury, and maybe beyond. Perhaps this line would pass through interesting places and do interesting things. It all seemed 'rather exciting'. He got together with Paul Broadhurst, and between them they hatched the plan to track the line across the countryside and document their findings. Given the distance involved this would require the journey to be undertaken by car, making stops on the various roads and in the various towns that it crossed or passed through.

Hamish would dowse and drive, Paul would navigate, and the two of them would write up the whole endeavour. They felt it could take several weeks of work, but at the end of it there should be enough material for a book of some description.

Life, especially when dowsing is involved, somehow never quite pans out that simply. Hamish spent an intense period of training for the journey, making quite sure he could recognise the energy signature of 'John's line' amidst the background noise of a plethora of other energy sources and centres. Only when he was absolutely sure he could sense the target energy distinctly from every other vibration - and could do so blindfold - did the duo hit the road to start the project that was to result in *The Sun and the Serpent.* The work soon ran into trouble. Hamish dowsed and Paul plotted, but the resulting line was anything but straight. Tempers frayed, and the initial conclusion was that either Hamish was a rubbish dowser or Paul was a rubbish plotter. As we now know, neither of these assertions was correct. It took them a while to realise that when following the line continuously across open country, as opposed to just noting occasional crosses on the Ordnance Survey map where it crossed a road or track, John's line snaked its way over the landscape in a most serpentine manner. Not for the first time, and certainly not for the last, the dowser was humbled into taking a number of deep breaths, adjusting the paradigm, and starting again.

As the project got underway properly, it became apparent that the line passed through an improbably large number of places that had connections with the name or the actions of St Michael - and the Michael Line was born (well, at least it was given a name that brought it to the attention of the rest of us).

The catalogue of places they visited and the experiences they had along the way are well-documented in *The Sun and the Serpent* and it is not the purpose of this book to repeat those episodes here. Suffice it to say that the dowsing duo were a little surprised that Michael seemed to avoid so many obvious energy targets and sacred sites on the way east. It was also strange that where Michael did pass through a significant place, it seemed to behave strangely, as if it were dancing with an invisible partner. However, they could make no real sense of it until they reached the wondrous megalithic temple that is Avebury.

Even in its partly dismantled, partly reconstructed form, this is a site like no other in Britain. Even to someone like myself, who has visited it numerous times over the decades, from primary school outings to crop circle forays, it can still cause the involuntary drawing of breath. Even today, it evokes the direct link to a distant and dimly understood past, like nowhere else.

The caravanserai car journey of Hamish and Paul eventually arrived at the magnificent henge in May 1985. While dowsing the effects of Michael on the energy of the stones, and getting more and more confused, Hamish had one of those flashes of inspiration that are the hallmark of an open mind. He experienced the revelation that there was another energy line twisting around the first - equally sinuous, equally significant, but generally gentler and more mellow. This suddenly explained the missing of the major targets and the interplay of the two lines where they crossed. So, after several months, much accumulated wisdom and the odd fracas, they were right back at the start, tracing what came to be called the Mary Line across much of the same territory.

Hamish and Paul at the Cheesewring, Bodmin Moor

The two researchers continued to follow the two lines until they disappeared into the North Sea off Hopton in Norfolk (the lines that is, not Paul and Hamish). It was an astonishing undertaking and a groundbreaking discovery.

The story of the finding of the Michael and the Mary lines has inspired a whole generation of dowsers, myself included. It's a Boy's Own comic strip, a rather more esoteric version of Indiana Jones. But unlike popular science fiction - however gripping or addictive that might be - this read was for real. It became a book you could put down on the table, pick up whatever temporary device you could find at hand and go off to verify or refute its assertions for yourself - there and then.

For me, it had the added bonus that, unlike the legends of the Egyptians or the glory of Rome, this epic strode, like a mythical Arthurian knight, through great swathes of the countryside that I had known all my life. Reading this book was like finding a Worm Hole in the High Street.

It made Hamish into a cult hero, albeit one with a tiny following, and it assured them both of a place in the dowsing pantheon that it will be difficult for anyone to emulate. It wasn't so much <u>what</u> they found, although that was remarkable enough, but the fact that they realised that there was something <u>to</u> find. It opened up a niche in the force field, a crack in the encompassing wall - and it set the rest of us off on a journey that we would never have imagined possible without it.

It is this breakthrough that set Hamish Miller apart from others in the field and, despite all his subsequent insights, it will be this for which he will primarily be remembered.

On Scillonia

The Isles of Scilly are situated some 28 miles off the southwesterly tip of Cornwall. They are a magical place, even by Cornish standards, and there are numerous archaeological sites and sacred spaces that seem transcendentally timeless.

While the rest of the Scillies were, in times long gone, once joined together in one land mass - and to the Cornish mainland - a deep channel separates the most westerly of the inhabited islands, St Agnes, from the rest. Even in the age of the helicopter and the Internet, St Agnes is still a very special location.

**Hamish (right) and Donovan Wilkins (second right)
at the St Agnes labyrinth**

Hamish, Paul and the legendary Cornish diviner, Donovan Wilkins were recruited to give dowsing input to the reconstruction of the stone labyrinth facing Bishop Rock and the Atlantic Ocean beyond. Their handiwork can be inspected on the seashore by anyone visiting the island.

Some local people were concerned about the use of dowsers to identify the correct site for the rebuilding, but a comparison to an old photograph of the site subsequently showed that Hamish and his colleagues re-sited the stones that they found half-buried in the surrounding turf in exactly the right place.

From Ireland to Israel

The finding and documenting of the Michael and Mary lines set a chain of events in motion that would change both the scope and the image of dowsing forever. As if from nowhere, alongside the venerated diviner there was a new kid on the block - the Earth Energy Dowser. Certainly, there had been people researching this field for several decades, many doing sterling groundwork, but the establishing and the publicising of the long distance energy lines brought a whole new group of amateur enthusiasts into the fold.

Hamish at St Michael's Mount

Having found one 'domestic' pair of lines, the motivation to see what else was out there was immense. The next major project came about from Hamish's meditations at his favourite outdoor energy centre - St Michael's Mount, near Penzance in Cornwall.

As recently as mediaeval times this impressive, steep sided hill stood in the remains of a salt marsh, which has subsequently become part of the sea, now known as Mount's Bay. There is a strong visual comparison with its sister site on the coast of northern France - the causewayed Le Mont St Michel - and with Glastonbury Tor in Somerset, the mythical Isle of Avalon, which was also surrounded by extensive mires well into historical times. All three are legendary sacred sites and powerful energy centres and all three are connected by strong energy links.

Hamish was used to the energy on the Mount and knew the signature of the Michael and Mary lines intimately. However, he became aware that in the epicentre of the energy whirlpool, there were more than just his two old friends pirouetting. Two other energy lines, just as strong, but with a subtly different feel, had come out to play. After some local research, it became apparent that these too were long distance lines that crossed West Cornwall at an angle and seemed to be heading off towards Ireland to the north west and across the English Channel (or La Manche, depending on where you are standing) to France in the south east. Did other countries have this energy too? Could energy lines really cross oceans? He was about to find out.

The project that became *The Dance of the Dragon* required a completely different level of logistical planning and made their previous exploits look like something of a tea party. If lines could cross continents, then serious amounts of travelling time would need to be set aside and appreciable sources of finance would need to be marshalled.

This expedition was very different in many ways, not least because the demon duo were joined by their partners in the venture - Ba Russell and Vivienne Shanley. This brought a different dynamic to the dowsing and a changed perspective to the expedition.

The itinerary eventually took them from Skellig Michael off the west coast of Ireland, through Cornwall, the Channel Islands, France, Italy,

Hamish, Ba, Paul and Vivienne

Greece and finally to Israel - ending enigmatically at Armageddon.

The catalogue of exploits and discoveries of the fabulous foursome is described in great detail in the trans-European travelogue that became *The Dance of the Dragon*.

Doubtless following in the footsteps of hundreds of others, who were energised by this book, I have sought out parts of what became known as the Apollo and Athena lines myself in various parts of Greece. Dowsing at the Acropolis, amongst the hordes of tourists, was an experience in itself - with children of various nationalities asking in their native tongues 'What's that funny man doing,

Daddy' and doubtless getting the usual response along the lines of 'Don't worry, he's just an eccentric Englishman'. At one point, I was asked to stop dowsing by an official guide, the only time this has ever happened to me to date, 'in case I damaged the stones'. Given that this is a site that has been blown up by Napoleon and used as an ammunition store by the British, I didn't think my two bits of bent wire could do much harm . . . but maybe I was just part of the fall-out from the Elgin Marbles debacle. However, I had a secret weapon, literally hidden up my sleeve - and I finished off the dowsing deviceless.

Dowsing down under

Through one of those improbably unlikely chains of events that seem to happen to people who have opened their minds to such things, Hamish and Ba were invited to try their hands at dowsing for earth energies in New Zealand.

As with most major dowsing expeditions, what you see often bears very little relation to what you get. If they had thought this might be a Technicolor antipodean version of the previous enterprises, they were in for a great surprise.

For a start, the long distance energy lines that had characterised the European adventures were nowhere to be found. There <u>were</u> earth energy lines, as there are all over the world, but the complex interplay between them seemed sadly lacking. Whereas the intersection of major lines at the Hurlers on Bodmin Moor, or at Avebury, produced both elegant spirals and something akin to an invisible kaleidoscope of petite pictures, the equivalent locations in New Zealand initially demonstrated very little of note.

Eventually, they did come up with some interesting earth energy patterns and, after much effort, Hamish was able to dowse a mundane manifestation that resembled a dog bone. This pattern morphed, more rapidly than similar transitions in the old world, into a beautiful floral design. Eventually, Hamish dowsed a manifestation that looked like a circle of origami figurettes. Interesting though this seemed, it was evidently not destined to be the focus of the expedition.

The major breakthrough of what was to become a five-journey saga, was the discovery of the inter-relationship of dowsing, energy, spirituality and the sacred sites of the ancient people of those southern lands.

Barry Brailsford

Most of us are aware that there were indigenous people in New Zealand before the Europeans arrived, and that the colonial period was a pretty miserable one for them - as it is for any people in any occupied country. The story that Hamish found, however, like a picture within a picture, was that the people the settlers dispossessed were themselves usurpers of an earlier indigenous culture. That culture, the Waitaha, had a highly developed philosophy that had freed them from conflict and the need to make war. When the more aggressive Polynesians arrived, they were sitting ducks.

The destruction of the Waitaha civilisation has been carefully documented by Hamish's new partner in time, the renowned social and spiritual historian, Barry Brailsford. He describes a people who were so closely in touch with their higher selves that they chose to be killed in great numbers rather than to fight back and risk losing their access to a greater reality. This is faintly reminiscent of the more recent episode of the native Tibetans who were maltreated and imprisoned by the Chinese. Their greatest fear was not in being killed or even dispossessed, but that in their anguish and their pain they might lose compassion for the invaders - and, in so doing, be themselves deprived of the portal to the next stage of their journey. It was the ultimate trial of their belief.

The exploration by Hamish, Ba and Barry of the special sites and the sacred places of the Waitaha is documented in the beautifully presented and illustrated book *In Search of the Southern Serpent*.

What they did find were the traces of a culture for whom the landscape was alive; a people for whom the veil between the energy of a place and its physical presence was paper thin; a way of thinking where documented history, living legends and the features of their homeland were entwined at every level of understanding.

For those who know something of the Aboriginal people of Australia, some of this will seem slightly familiar. Although their culture has been extensively deconstructed over the last couple of centuries, it is now believed that the Aborigines maintained and developed their unique way of looking at the world for over 10,000 years. To them, the countryside, their history, their legends and their understanding of the non-physical merge into a subtle soup that those of us more used to the printed word and history you can hit with a stick, find difficult to penetrate.

Seemingly the Waitaha in New Zealand thought along similar lines, but as their culture was swept away long before the arrival of the White Ghosts, it is as if their spiritual awareness has been preserved in aspic. Astonishingly, a few descendants of these earlier native New Zealanders still live on, away from the public eye, and their discussions with Hamish and Barry make fascinating reading.

Perhaps the most incomprehensible attribute of the Waitaha was their reputed ability to create their own reality, which we will discuss later on.

Call of the East

No account of Hamish's epic dowsing sagas would be complete without a mention of the visit to Russia in 1991. Hamish and Ba joined a group of

Hamish and colleagues dowsing in Russia standing next to an extension of the Mary Line

UK dowsers who had been invited to join fellow researchers behind the Iron Curtain, just as the former USSR was disintegrating. Whilst there, the group worked with professors of physics, geology and geophysics on various earth energy projects. Hamish was surprised to find that a considerable number of Russian academics had always taken dowsing seriously. For many of them, it is not a New Age revelation, but a well-accepted part of the process of becoming a professional engineer. Hamish was even more astonished to find that some Soviet professional courses taught dowsing, and even required a competency in it, as part of obtaining a qualification.

Our trip took us to Vyborg, north of St Petersburg, close to the border with Finland. I realised that we could be crossing what we would call the Michael or the Mary lines, somewhere near there - based on a line I had projected on a map. We found it, jumped out of the bus into several feet of snow and had our photo taken. Some of the Russian members of the group also found the line, and became very excited about its implications.

Perhaps we should not be so taken aback by the interest of our Russian colleagues in the information gleaned from wielding rods and pendula. As long ago as 1970, *Psychic Discoveries Behind the Iron Curtain,* by Sheila Ostrander and Lynn Schroeder, was published under the Abacus banner. This book contains a short chapter on dowsing, as part of a more general introduction to Russian investigations into psychic and pseudo-scientific phenomena, and briefly attracted the attention of the tabloid press in the UK.

During a visit to Novorossiysk, on the Black Sea coast, and to Moscow in 2006, Ros and I were able to carry out some dowsing without fear of arousing suspicious attention. It was quite apparent that many Russians had at least heard of dowsing and regarded the process as pretty matter-of-fact. Although we did not have the time to dowse the interior of St Basil's in the heart of Moscow on our stopover, it struck me that the spiral nature of the Cathedral's domes seemed to echo the energy patterns often found at large sacred sites. Were these really coded statements of the presence of the earth goddess or of natural energy vortices? I even wondered if the vibrant colours of the strands of the domes' ornamentation could correspond with those of the interference patterns generated by the underlying earth energy lines.

Hamish presenting his sculpture to the Metropolitan of Kiev Cathedral

During his visit, the Bo'ness Blacksmith was able to achieve a personal high point. Hamish had made a scaled-down metal sculpture of the cover of the Chalice Well in Glastonbury - allegedly the first Christian Church in Wessex (now part of England). This he presented to the Metropolitan of St Sophia's Cathedral in Kiev, which stands on the site of the oldest Christian church in Russia (now in the Ukraine).

Water divining

Unlike most other well-known dowsers, HM's published work makes very little reference to the whole subject of water divining. Yet, during the whole of the 400 years of the suppression of dowsing under the Witchcraft Act, it was only the vital knowledge of water divining that kept alive awareness of the innate skill, at least in public. I found this a little strange, but I suppose it all depends on how you get into dowsing in the first place. As we have seen, Hamish started as an earth energy dowser and moved on from there in an even more philosophical direction.

> Quite frankly, I've done comparatively little water divining - and I'm not very good at it, actually. When I wanted to have a borehole dug on my own land, I got a specialist. I have to confess that I had found a couple of places that could have been suitable for a borehole, but neither of them was the place that the specialist selected.

> I assumed that a professional water dowser would search out and find pure water. That turned out to be a bit of naivety on my part, because although he did find a source of water, if I had wanted to use that water, I would need to have put in a filtration plant for three and a half thousand pounds. Now, I thought they would have asked all the relevant questions, such as 'Is this water drinkable, is there too much aluminium, iron, arsenic, etc?' But apparently, that's not the standard practice, and it surprised me a little.

Hamish may have been a bit unfortunate in his choice of diviner, as all the professionals that I have ever come across would determine whether water was potable as a matter of course. In a domestic situation, there wouldn't seem to be much point in drilling for it if it wasn't drinkable!

> The local water divining legend here in Cornwall is, of course, the late Don Wilkins - he was fantastic. He found water with a 94 per cent success rate, which is phenomenal. Whether all of it was drinkable, I don't know, he never actually told me the story about what happened afterwards!

One of the usual assumptions is that water divining and the locatic
sacred sites tend to be part of the same process. Indeed, most dow
feel that you can't have a sacred site without an integral 'water fea\
Hamish was not convinced that this assertion should be taken at fac
value.

> I don't feel that the presence of a water line is necessary to
> define a sacred energy centre. You will find water, perhaps
> some distance away, but not necessarily within the site itself.
> It is much more likely that the site became sacred because
> most of the time it was itinerant people who visited it. It felt
> good to be there because of the underlying earth energies. If
> there was a source of pure water fairly close, it would
> become a place for them to stay. If they stayed for a while,
> and undertook their own ceremonial activities, the earth
> would have responded. Consequently, the centre became
> more powerful and a sacred site was created.

The greatest public failure

As a result of his growing reputation, HM was asked to take part in an
early episode of the very popular Channel 4 Sunday teatime archaeology
programme, The Time Team. The producer of the series was very open
to the idea of dowsing and Hamish was asked to dowse for a lost
processional path to a fogou (underground passage) near Lamorna Cove.

Hamish and Ba did their stuff quietly and produced a sketch map showing
where they felt the path had once been. Part of it traversed land off limits
for confirmational digging and part of it ran through a stand of trees,
which couldn't be probed by geophysics. When the geophysicists did
find something on Hamish's sketch that looked like a reasonable target
over which the professional archaeologists could put in a trench, it failed
to produce anything historical.

> Eventually, they found their own place to excavate, but after
> they had dug down about six feet, all they could unearth was
> an aged, rusted water pipe - which I thought was very funny.

As so often when put to the test in the full glare of publicity, dowsing
refused to play ball.

Hamish was clearly upset that two of the main members of the team were
openly hostile to the idea of using a dowser at all, refusing even to speak

to him. This must have had some bearing on his ability to be objective
and impartial during the dowsing process - and it put him under pressure
to produce hard evidence.

> I couldn't get into dowsing mode at all with the tension
> associated with their expectation of results.

However, the presenter, Tony Robinson, was open-minded enough to
give it a try and asked Hamish to make him some dowsing rods, with
which he had some initial success. The Wiltshire archaeologist Dr Phil
Harding was gracious enough at the end of the process to accept that he
felt that HM had indeed located the correct line of the path, at least at a
point immediately adjacent to the fogou, where the retaining wall seemed
to be of a later date to the rest of the structure - so Hamish was able to
leave the set not entirely crestfallen. It was, however, an object lesson in
humility.

> It was my greatest, most public, failure (laughter)!

In hindsight, he felt that, as ever, things worked out for the best. If he had
been dramatically successful on that first occasion, his next few years,
that proved so valuable in terms of practical research and personal
development, could have taken a radically different and media-managed
course.

If there is an example anywhere in this book of how Hamish approached
his world with the utmost integrity and seriousness, but didn't take
himself with any seriousness at all, it is this cameo event. For anyone
with even half an eye on his personal future, status or regard, this would
have been a catastrophic come-uppance. Some might even have tried to
prevent their part in the programme being broadcast at all, given the
unreasonable circumstances surrounding the failure to find anything
meaningful. To Hamish, it was little more than a bit of wry humour,
played on him by forces unknown, which helped him to stay on the
unseen path, rather than to be drawn into a realm where he would have
learnt little - and perhaps could even have been drawn back towards the
goals of his previous life.

No party trick

I was always taught that dowsing is not to be treated lightly. By all
means use it to demonstrate the potential of the process - which might
involve using it for things that are pretty trivial. However, always

remember that the force you are investigating, and with which you are interacting, is one that is connected to a more profound understanding of life itself.

This is not the universal view. I have seen many dowsers, experts as well as just novices, who understandably feel they have a new gadget to play with and apply dowsing to everyday activities. There is a school of thought that this is, in fact, how you get to be a decent dowser, by using it all the time, even for effectively meaningless activities. This strand of thinking supports the idea that by using dowsing for mundane things, we operate in a safe space. When we have mastered the basics, we can then move on up to delve into ideas that do need more considered concentration.

One situation that is always a strict no-no for the dowser is showing off. Try to use the skill to show how clever you are and you will fall flat on your face. I can vouch for that personally and, arguably, Hamish's Time Team nightmare was just such a bucket-of-cold-water event. As ever with dowsing, you have to do what you think is right, but that can vary from person to person and from time to time. Even Hamish and Ba didn't always agree:

> I'm a bit sceptical about using dowsing for everyday events like finding somewhere to park the car, although the way some people do it, it seems to work. Ba does it all the time. When we go shopping in Penzance, Ba will ask for one space, please - and just as we're coming down the top of the road, somebody will be getting into their car and driving out. I don't actually see anything wrong with that. But really these are frivolous things and I don't like dowsing being used for frivolous things. I don't like to see people going into Tesco and dowsing over columns of cheese, all of which are identical. I think it's possible that they are kidding themselves. Dowsing is a serious intuitive skill; it's not a party trick.

> There's a perfectly logical argument that someone else's need might be greater than your own and therefore you shouldn't ask, pray or dowse for things for yourself. On the other hand, if you go along with the sense that the gods are with you, and the universe is with you, and nature is with you - and they provide you with a parking space, it's yours - and you should accept it with grace.

In the day-to-day world, you should use your sense of gnowing (realising that you understand without any physical evidence to corroborate your intuition). There's an argument that your sense of gnowing is a type of internal dowsing. I think that that is the process we should be using all the time. To get out a physical dowsing rod and deliberately dowse for little things, you run the risk of getting to the stage that you are incapable of making your own decisions. You'll end up saying 'shall I have a boiled egg this morning? I'd better get the rods out'. That's a nonsense. That's the sort of thing you should gnow about. 'Does your body want an egg - I can absolutely guarantee that my dowsing response is YES - TWO - every morning'.

When and where dowsing is advisable - and also when it isn't - is addressed formally by the British Society of Dowsers code of ethics (see Appendix A). Further, it is standard practice amongst most dowsers to ask three questions before commencing a dowsing session or working on a particular site - Can I? May I? Should I? However, on some occasions just about every dowser gets a 'no' to one of these questions. When this happens, it's time to stop. If you don't, you'll tend to get either random responses or nothing.

The whole debate about when and why the dowsing response is denied, or when it just cuts out, could be a book in itself. Is it that something outside of you intervenes, like a teenager being grounded for breaking a

mutually agreed bond by coming home too late? Or is it that something inside of you, which some would call a conscience, or a sense or foreboding, cuts in to prevent you getting into deep water, and to keep you on your own internal path. This latter view would indicate that we do have an instinctive, impersonal view of right and wrong, at least in a given set of circumstances, which probably opens up yet another portal on the reader's rapidly destabilising world.

Pictures in the Ether

One of the fascinating insights into Hamish's dowsing career has been the rediscovery, with a little prompting, of pictograms manifested in the earth's energy field. These little figures, which can have an eerie resemblance to the logos of organisations and companies, not to mention the symbolism of major movements and philosophies, can be dowsed at a wide range of significant places on the earth energy grids.

I can't imagine how anyone would come to understand that such obscure phenomena could be there, other than through sheer intuition, but I have been able to verify them myself by asking if there are any of 'Hamish's little pictures' nearby. On receiving a yes, like any other dowser of modest ability, I can then follow the rods to the designated place and trace them out on the ground. A few examples of the pictograms, drawn from the vast library of the Miller Files, are shown overleaf.

Invisible images

Hamish himself was very clear that the only reason he knew to dowse for the pictograms was due to the work of his own mentor, Colin Bloy. Colin found them at significant places during the time he was running the Fountain Group in Sussex.

> I didn't believe him at first. We were walking down a pavement in Brighton, and he showed me the shape of a 'Cross of Lorraine'. I'm very sceptical about these sorts of things, so I waited until he had gone, and I dowsed it for myself. To my great surprise, I found - not exactly the same shape - but a very similar sort of thing.
>
> It was actually manifesting a shape, a simple shape; it seemed as if it was a form of contact with the Earth itself. I felt it was an attempt to establish a method of communication between two enormously disparate species - the earth as an entity, perhaps akin to Lovelock's concept of Gaia, and a human. How could we communicate - by symbolic shapes, through mathematics, using sound . . .? I found the whole concept very difficult to comprehend.

I can find little reference, even to the very existence of these energy features, in mainstream dowsing literature. This seems surprising, given the prominence afforded to other similar enigmas. Hamish worked with them for so long that they became just another part of his esoteric landscape. However, I couldn't help thinking that the room I inhabit, which once seemed quite well understood, if a little cluttered, had just acquired another pair of patio doors leading into an unexplored garden.

The illustrations on the next few pages give an indication of some of the vast range of types of pictograms Hamish was dowsing, recorded by Hamish himself on graph paper.

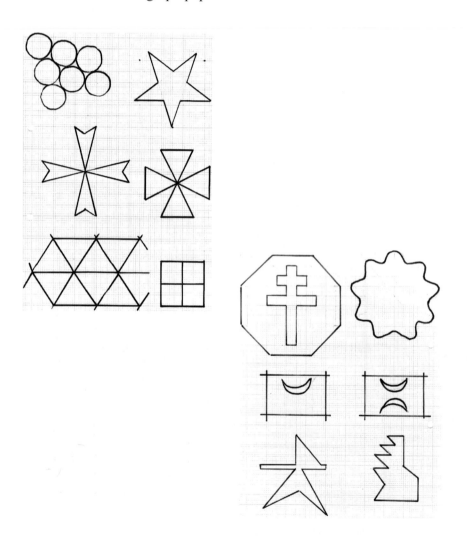

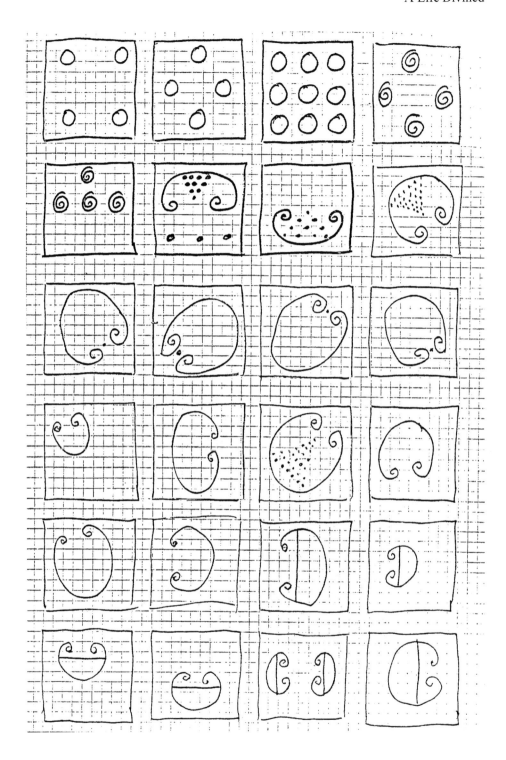

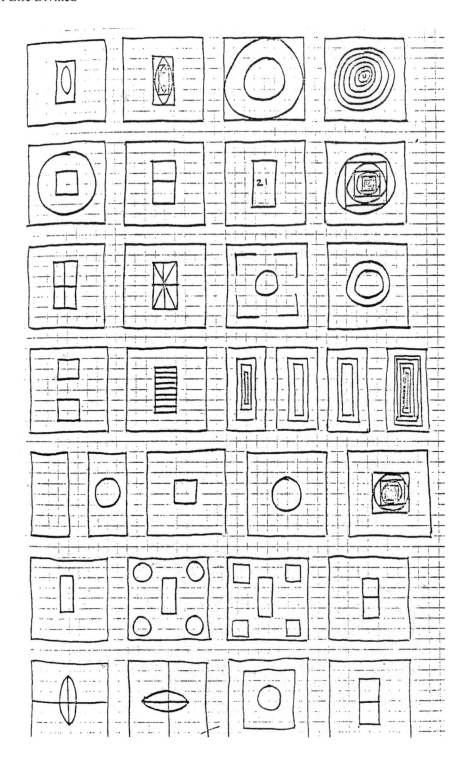

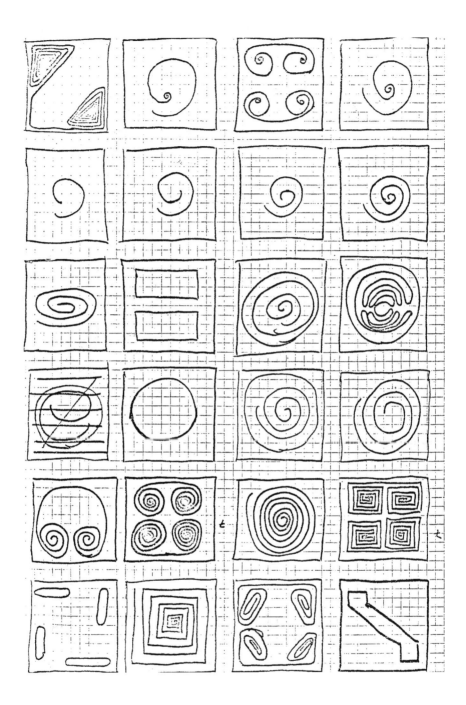

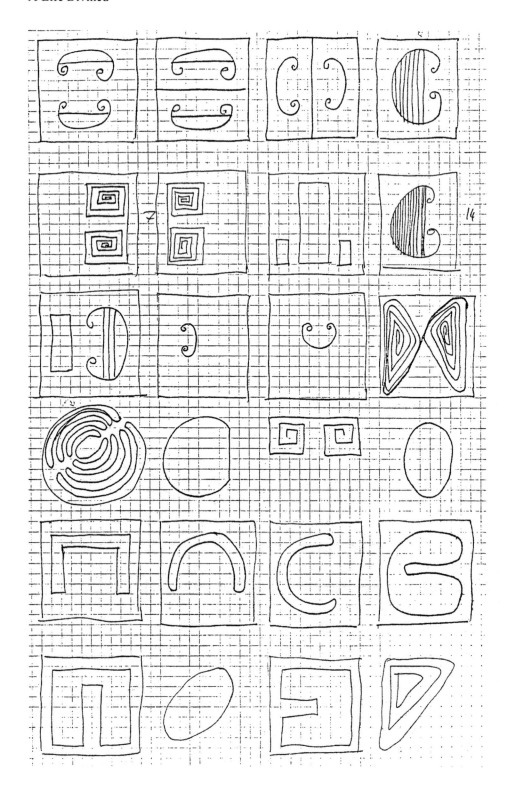

DOWSED WITH HAND ONLY 46

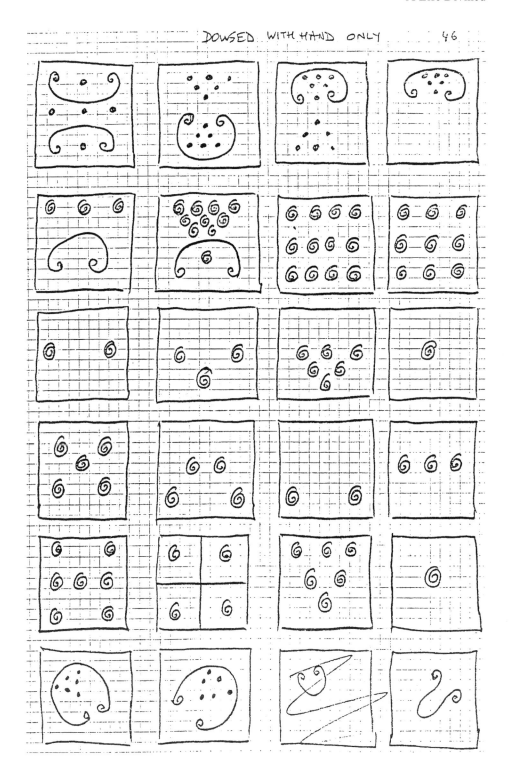

These are just a tiny sample of the sketches from the 'Miller Files'. There's page after page of them. You feel that if Hamish had carried on, he might have dowsed and drawn indefinitely. The range and scope of the forms and shapes is quite bewildering. Their origin mystified even Hamish and almost three decades later he was little wiser.

However, the finding of these forms at sites of energy interference would imply that the shapes are inherent in the way energy interacts with our environment. Because some of these symbols are used throughout the world, people may well have been aware of them for a very long time. This, in turn, could have had an enormous bearing on the development of symbolism in society. We make an assumption that a logo is invented and that it comes into existence at that stage, but these pictograms indicate that such forms have existed as long as there has been energy, and certainly long before humans. Despite their futuristic graphics, they seem to be natural energy patterns that have in some way been transposed into society, or certainly into our mental awareness. In putting them on to paper and on to the computer screen, they have developed a physical format as well.

> . . . and we're talking about just one flat plane, dowsed on the ground, but these shapes are multi-dimensional; they have colours and sound and different frequencies. We're just scratching the surface of this.

As ever, it's that first scratch that actually makes the big difference. If you paint over a mural, the mural is gone. However, if someone else, at some later date scratches the covering paint, perhaps by mistake or intuition, they suddenly become aware of a wonderful multicoloured picture beneath it - one that they never had any inkling even existed. While almost all of the time is spent meticulously uncovering the lost antiquity, it is that first scratch that is the revelation.

> . . . and a painting is a two dimensional thing. If you rediscover a three dimensional piece, you have something nearer to what we are revealing with earth energy.

The graffiti of Gaia?

Having established that energy pictograms occur in various places, what could they be? The comparison to modern-day icons can be a bit misleading, as these tend to be constructed and developed from previous symbols and ideas. With the predominance of the pictograms at sacred sites, such as stone circles, it is tempting to attribute them to the original designers or developers of those places, who might have left a kind of energetic signature - 'Dave the Druid built this temple'. This would liken them to the mark left on paper by a Chinese chop. But again, this seems to be a case of looking through the wrong end of the telescope. There is no indication that cavemen, or cavewomen, signed their works - they just 'were'. Even modern designers and Masonic architects tend to leave their identification signatures in the structure itself, not in the energy matrix nearby (on reflection, maybe someone ought to check that there are no pictograms adjacent to the Gherkin or the Pompidou Centre!).

The other possible source of the pictograms, which leads us deep into the uncharted philosophical wilderness, is the idea that they are purely natural phenomena - natural features of the energy field. Because they have been used and remodelled over the millennia, it is difficult for us to see them as anything other than man-made. Perhaps our own sense of self-importance and egocentricity makes it even more difficult for us even to consider that these invisible hieroglyphs could be produced independently from ourselves.

However, there is an indication that that might indeed be the case. It also gives a potential source that Colin Bloy could have become aware of, however indirectly. Hamish takes up the story:

Jim Lyons

The Yorkshire dowser and engineer, Jim Lyons, introduced me to the Dutch-Swiss mathematician Daniel Bernoulli who was working in the late 1700's. Bernoulli was fascinated by the Fibonacci spiral and other natural mathematical phenomena. For some reason, he worked out what would happen if an intrusive magnetic field affected a Fibonacci figure. It's an impressively esoteric thing to even consider, but what he found was that it created shapes like petals and stars, which are very common in 'Colin Bloy's pictograms'. This guy worked this out around1780, and suddenly what

we've been doing for the last 20 years seems to have acquired some validity, because it looks like what we are actually picking up is the interference pattern of an energy line coming into a spiral. I had never heard of Daniel Bernoulli, or his predictions, until Jim Lyons told me about him.

There is clearly a danger in rushing to conclusions here, but it does point to some intriguing lines of research.

Daniel Bernoulli

As we saw in the previous chapter, when two simple, natural, energy lines cross, we invariably find a spiral of some kind. Some are more complex than others, depending on where they are and on what type and strength of energy we are dowsing, but they always produce an energy picture that any dowser can find. I have one in the kitchen; I expect you have one in your house too. They are found everywhere, not just at sacred and ceremonial sites like Stonehenge and Chartres. So, if this well-understood interference pattern is so matter of fact, could other interference patterns also manifest themselves in this manner?

The interface between the energy fields and the more material world displays a vast range of seemingly everyday shapes, which may be little more than organic reactions to the interplay of force and form. An example of this effect in action, which we take for granted, is the remarkable myriad of shapes created by the crystallisation of frozen water into snowflakes. The work undertaken by Dr Masaru Emoto in Japan, showing the impact of subjecting water molecules to energy interference, is seminal in understanding this process - and we will discuss the implications of his work later.

If the production of such enigmatic patterns is a natural by-product of such everyday events, the discovery of similarly profound organic shapes at the intersections of the energy matrix is actually not that surprising. The fact that the pictograms are found in great profusion at designated sacred sites where, almost by definition, various types of energy lines cross, adds circumstantial evidence to the idea that these shapes are just another type of interference pattern. That we have subsequently used them so extensively in other spheres of human activity, especially in the written work of the post-Caxton period, could be obscuring our view of them as natural shapes and phenomena that are integral to the essence of life itself.

Get your head around that! Hamish was trying - but he has had to leave it to the rest of us to figure out.

Given the wide distribution of the pictograms and the bewildering array of their form, it is of course possible that the entire energy ether around the globe is impregnated by this endlessly modifying field of shapes. It may be that it is only where the energy lines interact that they are highlighted sufficiently to be brought to the attention of the enquiring observer. Material for yet another Miller-inspired project.

Pictograms that grow

Without trying to stretch a tenuous concept too far, it does lead on, almost inevitably, to a consideration of those other enigmatic pictograms of the modern world - crop formations.

I had the good fortune that my in-laws chose to retire close to a Wiltshire village that, at the time, was almost unknown outside the immediate area - Alton Barnes in the Vale of Pewsey. It was, and still is, a peaceful, picture-postcard English village where, blissfully, not a lot goes on. Except of course in the summer, when hordes of visitors descend on the local pub from all over the world to get a glimpse of the latest shapes that have emerged in the surrounding fields.

For those of you who are interested to know more about this fascinating subject, there are a number of good books on Crop Formations, some of which are listed in the Further Reading section at the back of this book. In summary, for the benefit of anyone who has been living on the International Space Station for the last few decades and may have missed the news altogether, pictures have appeared in fields of growing crops every year for several decades in certain places in the UK - and most notably in Wiltshire. As someone with both an academic interest and some hands-on experience of the phenomenon, I can assure the reader that these really are 'something to see, and sense, before you die'.

Some of these patterns are clearly the work of people who like to create shapes in the fields, much to the understandable annoyance of the local farmers. Even the more precise pictures made in this manner tend to be a bit rough at the edges, subtly inaccurate in proportion and dowse as something made by man, for man. A large proportion, however, remain unexplained. In these, the crop is bent but rarely permanently harmed. The shape gradually grows out over the season and all but disappears by harvest time. The only real damage to the plants is caused by croppie-tourists trampling down the corn.

Any dowser walking into a formation will soon sense the energy of the site and be able to determine if they were made by artistic skill and enthusiasm - or otherwise. The unexplained ones usually arrive overnight, in the shortest hours of darkness in the year and, as often as not, in potentially full-view of any insomniac local people. While there are many stories of buzzing in the air and lights in the sky, the formal link between these events and the shapes themselves remains unproven and unphotographed.

Many appear regularly close to the plethora of sacred sites in the area,

Crop formation - Wiltshire. UK

and/or on crossing energy, ley or water lines. Some are unbelievably beautiful, however they are made, and the unexplained ones in particular are both highly complex and deadly accurate. It is difficult to get away from the concept that these latter shapes were designed by some form of advanced intelligence, with access to a very hi-tech package of Computer Aided Design. Remember these pictograms appear in the dark, in a very short period of time, using mainly standing corn as a graphic medium. They can be accurate to within a blade of wheat, across a huge design whose geometrical complexity can only be grasped if you have a helicopter and a pretty good computer package of your own.

Don't be put off by the intermittent media hype and the boasts of the hoaxers, you need to see and to dowse them for yourself on the ground - and then come to your own conclusions. The comparison with the patterning of snowflakes is compelling; the comparison with the morphology of Miller's mystery shapes, beguiling.

The power of shape and form

We all know that shapes and symbols have great influence, directly or indirectly, on the world around us. If they didn't, the world of marketing would be a radically different bearpit. However, the assumption is that this is a process of association; that we associate a logo, a badge or an emblem with other ideas and concepts - and that this has an influence on what we think and what we do. What the Miller thesis suggests is that there could be a <u>direct</u> relationship between icon and action. The pictograms appear to be formed in the ether by the interaction of energy and matter. However, the pictograms themselves may also be able to affect that ether - and consequently the material world of which we are a part.

Anyone who has looked more deeply into the healing tradition of Reiki will be aware of the active use of symbols to effect positive change. Also, any number of people, even many of those who would consider most of the concepts in this book as groundless tosh, still choose to wear symbols in their jewellery and tattoos on their bodies as a form of power attraction or harm deflection. People think symbols work.

If it were the case that pictograms have an essence of their own, then the way we view them, and the way we use them in such a cavalier fashion, needs a fundamental review. This could well be the reason why secretive cults and mystery religions have often tried to keep the symbols of their power under lock and key - away from potential misuse by those they considered to be ignorant or malign. However, the ether is not something that can be contained in a casket or cave. If Hamish really has rediscovered this relationship in our time, then it is out in the world - and we will have to come to terms with it.

An anecdote, which describes this relationship in a quite trivial, but hopefully reasonably reverential way, is the story of the 'spiral water'. Some years ago, I was reading in *Dowsing Today* that people had been drawing a symbol on a piece of paper and putting it under a jug of water - to 'purify' it. It seemed a harmless little experiment, so we tried it. We set up two jugs of identical tap water - one we placed on the work surface; the other we placed on a trivet we had been given that just happened to have a nice painted spiral on it. We left them in the kitchen overnight to see what, if anything, might happen. In the morning, we drew a third jug from the same tap and we poured out a glass from each of them.

To our considerable surprise, they all tasted different. Now, you can make some rational sense of the difference between the one taken straight from the tap and the one that was left to stand, given the chemical haze that accompanies much of our mains water. After all, this very experience has spurred many people to take up the seemingly bizarre habit of drinking bottled water. However, the difference between the two jugs that sat side by side on the work surface, for just a few hours, was less easy to explain. I would not contend that this is a laboratory-controlled, double-blind scientific experiment, but as an exercise in the use of form with intent, it opens up some intriguing areas of research. Try it for yourself. You don't have to tell your mates about it, unless and until you find it works for you. Even then, be careful, or you might find them looking for your horn stumps and the vestigial tail!

Perhaps a better-documented and well-photographed example of the interplay of shape, form and influence is the work, mentioned earlier, of Masaru Emoto mainly undertaken in Japan. Masaru Emoto's research, going back to the mid 1990's, concerned the differences in crystalline shape between water samples taken from various locations and then frozen to produce ice crystals.

His initial thrust was fairly simple. Take samples of water from various rivers, lakes, glaciers - and domestic taps; freeze them in the fridge and photograph the resulting ice using a high-powered microscope. The result, as you might expect, was a library of beautiful hexagonal 'snowflakes'. However, as a Doctor of Alternative Medicine, Masaru Emoto had another objective - he wanted to investigate the impact of the pollution of water sources at a fundamental physical level.

He had no clear idea of what he might find, but the results surprised him - and have appalled just about everyone who has seen them. Water from pure-ish sources displayed clear geometrical formats - albeit with vast and unexpected variations. Water from more polluted sources produced increasingly degraded patterns, until those from the most damaged were barely recognisable as ice crystals at all. While the pictures of tap water from many cities, including London and Paris, show disturbingly deranged pictograms, the general direction of the research up to that point could have been broadly predicted.

Then Masaru had a 'Miller Moment'. Even his own staff couldn't quite understand why he decided to play music to selected samples from his collection of test tubes, but the effect was quite unexpected and seriously stunning. Identical samples crystallised differently when submitted to a blast of Bach, Beethoven, folk music or heavy rock. Now, music therapy has been on the alternative agenda for a long time, and is gradually gaining more mainstream recognition, but never has the impact of sound on water at a fundamental level been shown quite so graphically. Given that the human body is very largely composed of water, I leave you to draw your own conclusions.

Continuing in the Miller vein, Masaru Emoto then took his experiments one stage further, by writing Japanese words, which appear as abstract symbols to the western eye, on the side of the sample tubes. Again the resulting change to the crystalline structure was astonishing. Positive words and concepts seemed to promote healthy crystalline growth; detrimental ideas and symbols had the reverse effect.

The work briefly reached the mainstream western scientific press. But as it required a savage reconstruction of the current paradigm to enable any ready-made rational explanation to be applied, it soon faded from view in favour of more digestible discoveries.

Seemingly as a last throw of the dice in his 1999 publication *Hidden Messages in Water*, Masaru Emoto placed a photograph of the face of a happy child under a jug of water and examined the impact it made on the frozen output. Again the result was one of enhanced 'healthy' crystalline growth. Presumably, that picture could have been of an icon, or of a venerated symbol, or of a drawing of a natural energy spiral. I'll leave you to get out your electron microscopes to check.

The Earth is Listening

Dowsing and religion

Again and again, the travels of Hamish and his friends brought them into direct contact with sacred sites of all shapes and sizes, all creeds and all ages. From Bronze Age stone circles to 13th Century cathedrals, solitary Menhirs to sprawling monasteries, ornate temples to simple sanctuaries, wherever they went, they just kept on being led to sacred sites. Earth energies have clearly been important to people with a religious bent for as along as religions have been around.

In Britain, the deliberate policy of both the Celtic and the Catholic Churches to reuse, rather than merely to destroy, the sites of the old religion was a fascinating choice. They could so easily, over time, have swept away all the special places of the previous order. Instead, they chose to build over and to recycle the same sites - again and again and again. For us, it meant the location of huge numbers of pagan and prehistoric sacred spaces were preserved. Indeed, in many cases, such as the geometrical gothic extravaganza, they were gloriously enhanced. They are still there today, neatly mapped out in mediaeval stone architecture for us to investigate.

There are numerous examples of churches incorporating standing stones or built within pre-Christian henges. At Alton Barnes, the church still contains a prehistoric stone structure beneath the floorboards, with inspection covers provided for the inquisitive visitor to view its former incarnation.

Hamish dowsing at The Merry Maidens - West Cornwall

It seems inconceivable that the new religion was unaware of the energetic basis of the old. When you study the layout of the magnificent, masonically-designed cathedrals of the 12th - 14th centuries, their attention to the detail of the energy footprint leaves the dowser in no doubt that while these structures were built by devoutly religious people, they were also people who knew all about the serpent in the soil.

There are hieroglyphs in Egyptian tombs that seem to indicate that dowsers were in action at the time of the building of the pyramids, the holiest of the last resting places of the god-kings of the Nile lands. From my own dowsing experience at sacred sites elsewhere, I can personally vouch that there is evidence that the pre-Christian Greeks and the Tibetan and Thai Buddhists were just as aware of the energy imprints underpinning their temples as were their Celtic cousins.

No, the question is not 'Did the precursors of today's religions know about earth energies?', but 'Why, if those energies are just natural emanations, did they incorporate them so deliberately and so comprehensively into their devotional structures?' There was clearly something very special about the interaction between the energies and the sites - and/or between the energies and the people who frequented those sites.

A conversation with Gaia

I am not sure if James Lovelock - legendary articulator of the concept of Gaia - the earth as a living, breathing entity - has ever tried dowsing. He probably has. At first sight, Lovelock's contention that the world might be a distinct being, which includes ourselves but has a quite separate consciousness, is difficult to take on board.

Yet, if we take the scale of the interaction down a few notches, our own bodies are full of distinct living entities, making out a novel existence in our guts, coursing joyously through our veins or tucked away parasitically in all sorts of unmentionable places. These cells, enzymes and viruses are every bit alive and, if forced to do so, many can decamp and set up shop somewhere else, or rather in somebody else. We exist symbiotically with them. Do these minute entities have awareness? Are they sensitive to a stimulus? Does their energy respond to the grosser actions of the entity I call Me? On some level the answer has to be yes. So is it too big a jump to think that the planet, through its energy grids, might indeed be aware of us and may feel drawn to communicate - even if only to complain?

The jury is still out as to whether we might be considered constructive cells or a parasitic nuisance.

While it requires a huge conceptual leap, it is not completely beyond our comprehension to think of our big, blue bundle of energy, whirling through space, as having some form of awareness. It may not be self-aware in a human sense, but it may be a lot more aware than we have ever given it (or should that be her) credit for, to date.

There are a few very simple, practical exercises that even the novice dowser can undertake, which demonstrate this tentative relationship. They don't necessarily challenge your grip on reality (if you still have one), but they do show that there is some form of interplay between the dowser and the energy of the earth.

The case of the expanding energy

One of the simplest methods of interacting with earth energy was shown to me early in my alternative life by Alan Neal, the dowsing tutor based in the Tamar Valley. I was on a course in North Devon. The group decamped from the classroom to examine the energies around the church next door. We tuned in a bit, and then walked across the main door of the building at right angles, in a line. The instruction was to stop when our rods crossed. This we did - and our findings presented themselves as a rather ragged row. No problem, not bad for a start. We then went over to the other side of the doorway and repeated the exercise in reverse - which resulted in a slightly tidier row of dowsers, feeling a bit more comfortable with what they had found. So much for that; nothing very startling, but a bit of reassurance gained. We then went off to investigate other phenomena in the churchyard and about half an hour later returned to our original position by the main door, where we were again asked to walk across the doorway in a line. It was on the tip of my tongue to comment that we had already done this, but I didn't know Alan very well at the time and I didn't have the confidence to say anything. To our collective astonishment, we found that the line we were dowsing had expanded on both sides, not by a few inches, which could have been put down to sheer inaccuracy, but by several feet. How could this be?

You can do this at home. You don't need a church or a standing stone. Any line will do. I expect you have one in the house or the garden somewhere. Obviously, if the line is wider to start with - and Alan had clearly chosen something substantial that would easily demonstrate the point - then the effect is more obvious and more easily measured, but even a titchy linette will show you the same process in action.

We saw earlier that one of the eureka moments in Hamish's dowsing career was the realisation that every human, plant and 'thing' emits energy in a series of straight radial lines. He went on to find that these lines linked together in a coherent tapestry - a kind of planetary web.

What really moved the investigation on to another plane was the discovery that these lines also responded to him. As he dowsed, the radials increased in number and reach - stretching out to join nodes further away. It was not too big a leap from there to realise that the interaction with one line or node could actually transmit information in some form from there to the next node - and so on across great distances, providing there were no breaks in the chain.

Suddenly, a whole raft of new ideas came into view. Could this be the basis of the legends of ancient peoples who could communicate over long distances? Could this be how telepathy or remote viewing works? One of the great challenges in talking to Hamish, was that each discovery led not just to the next question, but into a whole new area of investigation. When reading one of his books, you keep coming up against concepts that weren't even on the agenda when the chapter started.

Communicating with the earth, both with and without his rods, was a trademark of Hamish's personal development. A few years ago, he was invited to take part in the annual Tavistock Sings festival - not that he, nor I for that matter, actually sang - but I digress. He was keen to dowse at the stone circle at Merrivale, near my adopted hometown of Tavistock, to examine the effect of a working ceremony, in this case dancing to welcome the arrival of the Beltane sunrise, on the energy of that circle.

Merrivale Stone Circle - Dartmoor

I hasten to add that you rarely have anything much to welcome visually at that time of the day in this part of Dartmoor, but fortunately earth energy operates regardless of the weather.

Unknown to him, I had decided to join in too. Unknown to me, he was one jump ahead. I turned up before dawn to work out the number of energy radials in the circle (lines that come out from the centre like spokes). There were about 14 of them. As the dancers arrived, but before anyone did anything meaningful, the number of radials started to climb - 18, 22, 26 - but as the dancing got going, the number of radials increased more quickly - 35, 42, 58 - drummers drummed, singers sang, dowsers dowsed and the radials broke though the 100 barrier, eventually plateauing out at over 130. I was amazed, but not as amazed as when I sent my findings to Hamish and I found that he had caught the circle 'at rest' by going there the night before. Although he counted a different numbers of radials, his count had also increased 10-fold during the event.

Since then, I've been out with the Beltane dancers several times and I have visited the circle, at different times of the day and different times of the year, on scores of other occasions. Each time, the radial count is different, which I feel is a function of who has been up there recently and what they have been doing. Each time it reacts to my presence by expanding the count, sometimes quite slowly, sometimes rather enthusiastically, and now - and I know this sounds just a teeny bit silly - it seems to react to my walking up from the car park. It seems to be responding to my intent to be there. I can no longer catch it 'at rest'. It seems to know that I am coming up the hill, and behaves like a kid whose best mate has just opened the garden gate. Can a moorland energy centre really have this level of consciousness? If so, what does it tell us about the potential for communication between different types of life-form? But don't take my word for it - dowsing is all about getting your intuition grubby. As Colin Bloy once said 'Do it yourself!'

If you read any of Hamish's energy line adventures, you will discover that the earth's response is not restricted to the gentle game of mental ping-pong I enjoy with the Merrivale energy centre.

The dance of the icons

During *The Sun and the Serpent* project, Hamish became aware of interference manifestations centred on major energy intersections. These were usually very simple at the outset, but changed in nature as the project progressed. As the dowsing became more sophisticated and intimate, so the patterns became more intricate and demonstrative. The changes seemed to be sparked by the interaction of the dowser with the energy - and if that really was the natural energy of the planet, then a remarkable form of communication was taking place.

Each of the books of the earth energy trilogy documents how the manifestations developed from quite simple forms to complex patterns. A modest misshapen pentagram, first found at Carn les Bôles on the Atlantic tip of Penwith, ultimately flourished into four concentric twelve-pointed stars on the Norfolk Coast; a simple shamrock shape first detected in Ireland morphed into a three-fold quatrefoil design by the time the dowsing reached Greece; and the aforementioned derisory dog bone shape found in New Zealand transformed itself into a twelve-petalled, three layered masterpiece by the end of the southern sojourn.

The Sun and the Serpent manifestations:

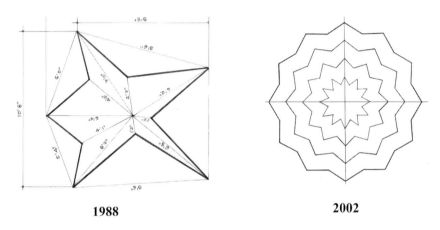

1988   2002

Dance of the Dragon manifestations:

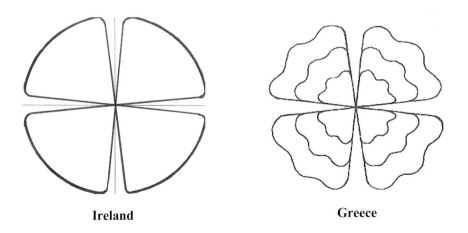

Ireland   Greece

As these changes can be detected right down the various lines, Hamish concluded that there is a form of communication all along the lines, as well as an interaction with the dowser. It became a hallmark of his work that this communication with what seems to be the earth itself, or at least some significant aspect of it, develops and matures. Simple, stylised icons morph into ever more complicated forms.

Hamish pulled no punches with his assertion that:

> There is an intelligent life form beneath our feet and it is communicating with us by means of dynamic symbols.

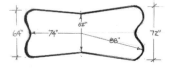

New Zealand - 'the dog bone'

New Zealand - the twelve-petalled masterpiece

New Zealand - last manifestation

It is important to note that both the pictograms described in the previous chapter, and also the manifestations discussed here, appear to be the result of the relationship of energy with energy, of energy with matter and/or of energy with the consciousness of the observer.

However, the manner in which this happens seems to differ between the two types of ethereal graphic. The pictograms do not appear to become more complex in themselves, but they may spread over time, increasing in number as they appear.

The manifestations however, remain at the same spatial coordinates, but become more complex as the observer interacts with them. The precise reason for this differential reaction is, to put it mildly, unclear.

These discoveries led Hamish to some of his most profound insights, and they prompted him to reconsider how cults and religions might have come to choose the sites and the symbols they have used down the centuries.

This is not to say that the ancient orders worked through the process of logo choice as, say, a modern marketing mogul might, but intuition is a strange phenomenon - one that we are only just starting to take seriously.

The Sense of Being Guided

The website of the Wyrd?

There are many millions of people across the world who, despite the wealth of material evidence to the contrary, insist on following a way of life that derives from the belief that something or somebody, somewhere, is pulling the strings of both their life and the lives of those around them. For many, it may be a part of their culture and their upbringing, and no more than that. For others, it is a deeply felt sensation that they are indeed being guided to choose one course of action over another.

There are few of us who do not, from time to time, go with our gut feeling, even when logic would dictate otherwise. Trying to analyse the relative benefits of these two worldviews would be almost impossible to tease out. In any case, unless you cling staunchly to one end of the spectrum or the other, the two are inherently intertwined.

Logic we can describe and understand reasonably well, but what exactly is intuition? One definition might be that it is the knowledge of a piece of information, such as the preferential outcome of an action, that could not be known to a person by direct or academic means alone.

There is clearly a huge debate as to whether intuition actually exists in any quantifiable form. However, given that just about everyone experiences situations where they have such a strong feeling that they ought, or ought not, to be doing something, we are drawn to accept that the phenomenon exists - at least in the mind of the chooser.

For Hamish the dowser, there was no doubt about the existence and the value of intuition. Every time we dowse, we are asking our intuitive self to access information to which, in concrete terms, we have no access. As dowsing has been shown to work, at least to some extent for almost all of us, so the status of intuition has been given a huge shot in the arm.

So, where does such a feeling originate? Hamish described it as an unspoken conversation with The Management. For others it is a dialogue with the divine. Yet, there is also the potential for it to be conceived as a more naturalistic process - in that you have direct access to an unimaginably vast database of information out there in the ether - and you subliminally sift through it using an incredibly powerful internal search engine that you never knew you had.

For those of a particular philosophical persuasion, it makes more sense to give this tendency a name and a form. As humans, we like to fashion our non-human support systems into virtual people, as this helps us to come to terms with them. So, our pets have names, our cars have names, our land has a name (and a gender) and somewhere further down the line the source of our intuition also gets a name and a whole raft of quasi-personal attributes - kindness, wisdom, vanity, anger, intention. This anthropomorphic process, as it is known, is one way of making sense of the unintelligible. It is a way of creating a reality we can live with - at least for the time being. Where the process starts to break down is when we actually start to treat these virtual people as . . . people.

Our intuition seems to be an innate ability that we have come to feel we no longer need. Today, we can do so much technically and mechanically that the application of 'second-sight' seems quaint and outmoded. Indeed, it has been on the back burner for so long, it has almost boiled dry. We are embarrassed to say that we appealed to it for advice on an important decision, and afraid to admit that we preferred to go with our feelings, rather than the rational advice of experts. Most of us have too little confidence in our own ability to actively put our intuition to the test in important situations - even when we can prove to ourselves that we can dowse intuitively with a demonstrable degree of competence.

However, for people like Hamish, intuition became part of an outlook on life and a practical assistance in dealing with the more intangible parts of it. This does not mean he eschewed the advice of his petrol gauge or refused to look up the weather forecast, but for everyday choices and guidance, he would naturally use his intuition as an additional sense, supplementing the wealth of scientific support that we have brought to bear on our ever more complex existence.

Yet intuition is only another tool, a process, like seeing or feeling. It is a means of tapping into another source of information, another type of data. The key to coming to terms with how intuitive dowsing might work requires another conceptual leap - this time to an appreciation of how that information might be stored, and therefore where it can be accessed.

There are a number of strands of thought that lead out from the acceptance that people are able to get hold of data to which they could have no direct contact. One of these is the idea that, in some form, everything that happens remains, apparently indefinitely, out there in the ether. It may not be on vinyl, or on celluloid, or on a smart chip, but it remains recorded in some form in the energy of the cosmos. This is the essence of the concept of the Akashic Records. If all of our actions, all of our thoughts and all of our intentions leave a footprint in the Energy Field, then under certain highly-specialised circumstances, we ought to be able to find that footprint.

This may well be a conceptual framework for the explanation of how dowsing could work, and it may also provide some basis for other seemingly inexplicable phenomena, such as remote viewing.

The turn of the wheel

Anyone who has a seen a past life regression in action, carried out under the supervision of an experienced practitioner, is likely to have been impressed by the sheer level of detail and sensation brought back into the present by the subject. Putting aside the debate about whose life is being accessed, the actual process leaves little room for doubt that the person being regressed is viewing a tableau of - and in some cases actually taking part in - a real or an imaginary previous event or situation.

In this context, Hamish closely followed the work of the Bristol-based researcher, Professor Peter Stewart. Peter has carried out a series of experiments whereby groups of people have been regressed to a point in time, often also when visiting a place of particular significance, and have then been asked to note down what they have seen, felt, heard etc. As ever with non-laboratory exercises, the accuracy of the data collected could be open to challenge, but the degree of consensus between the members of the group is often surprising. If this consensus were being realised by pure telepathy, that would be startling enough, but if it really is being uncovered by regression, then the implications would be astounding. I find the reported output of Peter Stewart's experimental subjects gains credibility as, more often than not, they appear in their personal experiences to be viewing the world-gone-by through the eyes of servants, peasants and bystanders, rather than embodying the roles of the major players in the scene.

> Peter has a theory of the permanence of information and the non-permanence of anything material. That makes so much sense to me. All we have to do is to find a way of tapping into it! That is so exciting. He has an amazing mind.

Part of his understanding of this permanent information is the continuance of the information that makes up the energy ball that is us – which some would call the soul. Words like 'soul' have been so overused in all sorts of inappropriate connotations that they have become devalued. However, call it what you like, Peter Stewart's interpretation of the phenomenon as the unending development of the information that we have accumulated makes a lot of sense to me, based on my own personal experience.

A further pointer substantiating this type of remote viewing, are the well-documented cases of people, particularly children, who have been able to show where they lived in a previous life - without any direct access to that information or to the place itself. Such reports, however well-documented, understandably tend to get put on a heap of miscellany for some future X-Files investigators to hoover up. This does not mean that the people involved were making it up. In most cases, they would have every reason not to do so, as they tend to end up being ostracised as weirdos and witches for their trouble. Such experiences fall so far outside the current paradigm, that they just cannot be willed or wedged into a recognisable place in the accepted structure. Either all of the children's accounts are fictitious or our existing worldview needs some radical reconfiguration.

If Einstein were alive today, I just get the feeling that this is the sort of inexplicable set of circumstances that he would be researching, rather than an ever more detailed and more expensive quest for yet another, even tinier, atomic particle.

Beyond intuition

In addition to having a potentially unlimited source of reference for our actions and our decisions, Hamish had a tangible sensation of being encouraged along a particular path. In holding this view, he was by no means alone.

Potentially, there could be two ways in which this could happen. Either there could be an external intelligence monitoring his progress like a sheepdog with a stray ewe, or he could have been drawn naturally, using his own intuition, towards an evolution that was in his own best interests.

Many people have an ill-defined sense of being guided by the drip-feeding of information. You can visit a dowsing site and come away with a few snippets of data that you have to go away and digest. You go back to the same site another day and you find a few more tiny pieces of the jigsaw. The original pieces were there all along, but you didn't find them. Applying rational thought to this process, clearly we all acquire information incrementally. The answer to each question opens up another line of research and so we progress. However, there does seem to be something unusual about how we discover certain things at certain times. It really can feel that you are being gently pushed along.

> That applied to me so often, particularly in the beginning stages with the work on The Sun and The Serpent project. I wasn't given the knowledge of the Mary line for about 18 months after I tuned into the Michael line. I just felt it was because if I had found them both at the start, I would have been so bloody confused, I would never have left Cornwall.

For my own part, each and every time I visit the Merrivale complex, I find something new. Often it's a trivial point, but it's been there all along and I've been to the site dozens and dozens of times before and not found it. It's as if it's time for me to become aware of that particular nugget of knowledge now. It makes no logical sense, but if I was easily spooked, I'd be well-spooked by now.

The stubbornly secular Hamish was in no doubt that he was being actively guided. His brief experience with The Management provided him with a potential mechanism for how this could have been taking place. However, this opened yet another can of worms. If The Management need the active participation of humans to enable evolution, how can 'they' be steering the lost souls towards the light? Hamish believed that this is all part of the inter-active process of creation, to which both humans and supra-humans contribute different abilities.

HM supported this view with a quotation, collected during his sojourn in the southern hemisphere, and attributed to an unnamed Maori elder:

'We are currently returning to a period of discovery of a psychic science, relating to the harnessing of earth energies. Some vestiges of this science have been preserved in many parts of the world by a few of the so-called 'primitive races', who still utilise the power emanating from sacred sites, which have lain partially dormant for many generations. The ancients mastered, to a very high level, a sophisticated psychic science, harnessing the world's elemental forces, together with a command of psychic power, far beyond anything we can, at this stage, even begin to comprehend. Many things are being revealed to us only in small fragments, lest we be unable to cope or understand what is to come.'

I feel that's a piece of extraordinary wisdom.

Holding the Other Rod

It takes nothing away from the work and the research that Hamish undertook, to state that he had more than a little assistance - and not just from 'the other side'. During his last thirty years, he worked in a whole series of collaborations with groups and individuals - and I feel privileged to have been one of those in a minor way.

He drew expertise and inspiration from many of those liaisons, and put a huge amount of himself and his insight back into them.

However, any account of the life and times of the dowser from Lothian must include a reference to his third wife, Ba, who was an equal partner in many of his most important endeavours.

This chapter is almost entirely in Ba's own words and it describes the extent to which the lives of Hamish and herself became intertwined.

Ba and Hamish Miller

On meeting a New Man

Blood relatives apart, Ba, a former physiotherapist, is just about the only person left alive who knew Hamish either side of his NDE:

> "I remember going to visit Hamish when he was ill and in hospital in Sussex, because Jean (his second wife) was down in Cornwall when he was rushed in. My then husband David came with me the night before he had his operation. I can remember Hamish being very resigned - he was lying there saying 'what will happen will happen' as we said goodbye and walked out.
>
> After the operation, and the NDE, he was moved to a nursing home - a halfway house before going home. I visited him, because he was walking in a very stooped manner, very protective of his gut, from which he had had quite a chunk removed. I remember, in my dreadful, bossy physio way, making him stand up and walk correctly, evenly, along the passageway.
>
> Not long after that came the enforced winding up of the company. By then, Hamish had changed completely and he didn't want to go on with that way of life anyway. He found it was no longer rewarding, and he had suddenly become aware of the beauty of the natural world - and how making all this furniture, and rushing up and down to London, was no longer fulfilling. So he decided to throw the whole thing up and move down to Cornwall.
>
> The complete change that Hamish had to put up with was quite eloquent. He'd had a powerful and elevated status; he had been running a big factory; he'd been used to having a big salary for some time - and he had a very smart car, which was taken from him at the time that the company ceased to trade.
>
> By the time we next saw him, he'd found a clapped out, old, orange Volkswagen. The lights on the front were half full of water and my sons, who were really wicked, drew goldfish on them. It was even a left hand drive car. But he was a resourceful chap and this gave him a means of transport to get down to Cornwall.
>
> We saw him from time to time, when he came back up to Sussex, but it was a complete and utter transformation - from being one of the country's high-rollers, to being on the dole.

One time, my family came down to Cornwall. We had an old boat and we sailed down to Falmouth. We came over to visit him in his home. Shortly afterwards, his wife Jean died - and Hamish lived on his own for about five years.

After my own marriage came to a crossroads, I spent some time sorting myself out by helping a friend who was going to turn a wonderful, but rather run-down house on the Isle of Skye into a retreat centre. I stayed there, looking after all the different renovations to the building, for almost a year. While I was up there, I had lots of time to walk and think - and in the end I decided to move down to Cornwall myself. I can remember the day I arrived, with a huge case of clothes and an even larger dog. Hamish was out and, as I was really tired from travelling, I lay down on the grass. I cold hear the wind in the trees, and I thought I could hear voices in the wind saying 'She's arrived, she's arrived'. I sat up bolt upright and I said 'Yes, I have arrived!' and I've never regretted it once."

The unlocking of the door

"The thing that set me off on my new path was something to do with Hamish. He came round one Christmas to visit the family - and he had with him some dowsing rods, which he had made in his forge in Cornwall. He gave me a pair of these rods.

He suggested to me that I should look for the strongest energy point in the kitchen, which seemed a funny thing to ask, but I agreed and I walked across the room. To my great surprise - the rods crossed! Hamish replied 'That's exactly right.' It set me off - it opened my mind.

We lived in a wonderful old rectory. It was attached to a little church, the original part of which was a tiny little one-celled cottage over 400 years old. It had been given to the Templars as part of a preceptory.

After Hamish had given me these rods, the family found that I would go off with them - and they started to complain that I hadn't made them a meal or done any washing up. I would go off dowsing and I would be in another world.

I remember one day walking into the church - we had our own passageway into it - and asking the same question. 'Where is the main energy focus in this church?' I thought the rods would go over to the altar, but no way, they took me down to where the choir changed, in a little room off a side aisle. I thought that was very odd. Then I did some dowsing on what had been a croquet lawn at one time, although it was rather neglected and a bit undulating. I started picking up shapes, which I also thought was very odd.

Hamish had told us how he had met Colin Bloy and that had got him started with dowsing seriously. Colin lived in Brighton, which wasn't far from Ashurst, where we lived, so I gave him a ring and asked for his advice. I asked him if he would come over and have a look at these shapes I had found. I added that he was welcome to tell me that they weren't there, that I should throw the rods in the river and go into a mental home!

He came out, did some dowsing, and then asked me for a piece of paper. He drew exactly the same shapes that I had found. I was astonished. So, I asked him to dowse for where he thought the main energy centre was in our little church. I didn't tell him what I had already found, but he walked in, and his rods took him to exactly the same place where mine had crossed - and he too felt that was very strange. Then he walked over to the altar and stood, and stood, and stood. I had no idea what he was doing. After a few minutes he declared that it had been sorted out. I didn't want to seem too sceptical, or to test what he had done while he was still watching, but the next morning, I went to investigate. Sure enough, the energy centre had moved and was then centred on the altar. When we looked at the old plan of the church, we found that the place I had found was where the altar had been located originally, but the energy had never been moved on to the new position of the altar."

"I began to realise that there was so much more to all this - and it was an amazing feeling."

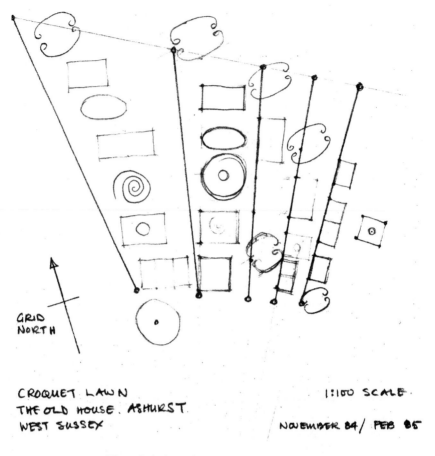

GRID
NORTH

CROQUET LAWN
THE OLD HOUSE. ASHURST.
WEST SUSSEX

1:100 SCALE.

NOVEMBER 84 / FEB 85

Plan showing pictograms drawn by Ba

The development of the dowsing duo

"I was dowsing up in Sussex, when Hamish was living down in Cornwall. He suggested that we did an experiment using the Fountain Grid, which was being used to send out love and healing to the areas around. In the grid, I would pick up certain patterns at my end, which were very similar, but never quite the same as the ones Hamish was finding in Cornwall.

When Hamish was investigating the Mary and Michael lines with Paul, I was still living in Sussex, so I didn't get very involved in that work. Although I did join them a couple of times when they were dowsing up in Wiltshire, because my parents went into a residential home near there."

"However, when I came down from Skye, I joined Hamish, Paul and Vivienne for the Dance of the Dragon project. I was in on that from the beginning."

"During the research on *The Sun and the Serpent*, Hamish had found it very exhausting to take on the dowsing of both the male and the female energy lines. So, we decided that I would deal with the male line and he would dowse the balancing female energy, especially as he had found that the Athena line, as we called it, actually ran through his forge! My role was to hold the male energy within me - but we always conferred on our findings, whenever I felt it was present. We would check each other's dowsing, but it was my responsibility to find the Apollo line in the first instance.

Ba Miller dowsing

Before we set off for the first leg of the journey, to Ireland, we went up to Gurnards Head, which is very close to our home near Lelant. It's where the Apollo line leaves Cornwall to go over to Ireland. I really felt I needed to get to gnow that energy deep, deep, deep within my being, so we all went up to Gurnards Head. I took off my shoes and I sat right on the very edge of the outcrop, facing Ireland. I meditated for a long time, to try to embody the energy of that line. After a while, I became aware of a kind of throb, not the sort you could hear - but I felt it in the very core of my being. I realised that it was essential that I remembered this feeling intuitively, as this would lead on to sensing the Apollo line throughout our European journey.

When we got to Ireland, we were going along a country road, and I began to think 'gosh, that feeling is coming over me'. It grew and grew, until it almost hurt in my chest. I said to Hamish that that male line was very close, but Hamish replied 'rubbish, it can't possibly be here'. He had the map; he knew where he was going and he knew where he thought the line should be - but I repeated that I was sure it was very close by. At my insistence, we got out of the car and dowsed until we found the place where the rods crossed. Hamish checked it - there was no doubt we had found Apollo. We climbed up a high bank beside the road and looked into a field. We saw that there was a dolmen, a cist grave, in the field. We investigated it and found that the male line had deviated from its expected course to go through the stone structure and then cut back to cross the road where I had first felt it. You couldn't see the dolmen from the car, so it was a huge confirmation of the accuracy of my dowsing.

Before we undertook each new tranche of the journey, I did a huge amount of research in the public library and elsewhere, to find out if there were any ancient places in quite a wide band around the next section of the route. I looked up anything of any historical interest, so that we would be able to cut down the time we spent abroad. You have to remember that we were all struggling financially, and that staying abroad for any time put quite a strain on our available resources. However, the more I did it, the more I seemed to be intuiting it. I had more time than the others, and I just loved doing the research. I acquired a hand-held voice recorder and I was able to record a running commentary, live, at each of the sites we visited. I was able to comment on physical and architectural features, but also descriptions of the energies we encountered. That really helped a lot when we came to the enormous task of writing the book.

The whole process took about ten years, on and off. We had to find the time to all be available at the same time, and we had to have the courage to commit to buying air tickets in advance, when we didn't have the money in the bank. The logistics were horrendous, but the end result was worth all the effort.

Hamish and I did the whole New Zealand project together, and that took another five years. There were various prompts to making the connection and eventually we woke up to the fact that we were being directed there. The original intention had been to find another pair of lines in the southern hemisphere, to compare and contrast with our previous work - but, try as we might, we just couldn't find them. I'm sure they are there, but we clearly weren't meant to find them. We got the feeling that The Management were telling us that we had been shown that earth energy lines existed, but it was now up to other people to do the travelling and the research on them - and to be enlightened by following these lines. We seemed to be being guided to go on and find something else.

The details of the journey are all described in *In Search of the Southern Serpent*, but it became a very clear direction to us that we were to understand, and to reveal, that the consciousnesses of both the earth and of ourselves are profoundly affected when they come together.

As part of our work in the southern hemisphere, we had the great privilege of meeting Credo Mutwa, the spiritual leader of the Zulu. We asked him about the lines we had found on the top of Table Mountain. He not only understood what we were talking about, but he astonished us by producing a map showing where they went - right the way up through South Africa, right up the East African rift valley, right up the Nile. Hamish and I looked at each other when he told us about them - and, fascinating though that revelation had been, we immediately felt, in unison, that it was not our destiny to follow those lines.

Although we didn't find the equivalent of the Michael and Mary lines in New Zealand, we taught other people to dowse while we were there - and they are finding earth energy lines that link together, which is great. I feel this is so important, because it introduced them to the understanding that the earth is alive."

Groundwork

"Another major undertaking that Hamish and I worked on together was the development of the land around Treviscoe, including the planting of over 1,500 trees, which are starting to mature."
"It was a huge undertaking, especially as I was still working at the time as a physiotherapist at the beautiful little hospital of St Michael's at Hayle. I hadn't intended to become a physio again, after I had left Sussex, as I'd done that for so many years. I had intended to do something completely different. However, I saw the advert in the paper, and it just seemed the right thing to do. It was a completely different type of job from the one that I had been used to doing in the South East. This was working for the NHS, whereas previously I had been a private domiciliary, working for a group of doctors, and going to people's houses."

Healing in tandem

"Well, at first I didn't see myself as a healer, as such, because it was so alien to my medical background. But I realised that physiotherapists, before any other medical staff, were the first alternative medical practitioners to be used in the NHS. We were recognised long before osteopaths and other professionals, who are now starting to be employed in the public sector. It was very pertinent that on our uniform badge there were a pair of hands and the sun - we used natural processes, and there were no pills or potions given out at all in our work. It was effectively healing using different waveforms, such as ultrasound and heat. Right from the beginning, I was never a great one for slapping machines on people. I was very much more attracted to the use of massage and doing things with my hands, which many patients actually remarked upon favourably. They often said 'You are the first physio that actually laid your hands on me.' So, I suppose, that healing was in me all the time.

It became a very important part of both of our lives."

Working in parallel

"We were both in at the beginning of the work of the Parallel Community. Hamish had sensed the message from the ancestors in New Zealand, about how they were so concerned about the damage we were doing to the planet - and to the prospects for future generations. From then on, we knew we needed to find an alternative way - a way of living a more peaceful lifestyle. However, we also realised that you can't knock something down without putting a credible alternative in its place.

This work has taken us on another huge personal journey - lectures, meetings, websites and newsletters, and lots of time spent stuffing things into envelopes. It's been an enormous commitment, especially at our ages. People thought we were totally loony to take it on. However, I think the universe is in favour of our efforts, because out of the blue, we've had so much help - it's way beyond coincidence."

On coming to terms with the NDE

When I came to write this section, I knew that for all her interest in dowsing and healing, Ba, like myself, had come from a very rationalistic background - in her case as a trained and grounded medical professional. So, I was interested to hear what views she had on the remarkable tale of Hamish's Near Death Experience.

> "I have found it very difficult to take it on board. I know he's not telling me a load of porkies, but my rational mind cuts in and I don't know quite what to make of it.
>
> My family are <u>totally</u> and <u>utterly</u> sceptical. My children are lovely, but when they come to visit they have very heated, but hysterically funny, arguments with us.
>
> Despite the books and the events described by his father, and all the lecture tours and accolades he has received, Hamish's own son, and his daughter-in-law don't have the slightest feeling that there is anything beyond the here and now. However, as I get to meet more people who have experienced NDEs, and to hear about more people who have been through them and survived, I have become more convinced myself that it is a real phenomenon - but I have to admit I took quite a lot of convincing!"

Hamish and Ba on their wedding day - 2005

Direction from <u>my</u> Management

Throughout the writing of this book, Hamish largely left me to my own devices. He prompted occasionally and contributed copiously, but he took the stance that my views were my own - and what I chose to include or exclude was my concern. However, one of the few issues that he was determined to see in the final version was an appreciation of the part in his own development played by Ba. I even wondered if I should, in fact, be recording the interwoven insights of the dowsing Millers, but it might then have been a very much longer book.

Hamish summed up the relationship:

> Ba is fundamental to my work. We heal together and we dowse together. She gets slightly different results from me, but that's because she's a female dowser.
>
> She's been a huge part of the development of my dowsing and of the logistics of it. The stability of my life is wrapped around her contribution.
>
> I'd like that contribution to be recognised - and not just in passing!

As we will now see, the Millers continued to work side by side, especially when it came to their own highly effective style of healing.

The Urge to Heal

Healing, in the non-medical sense of the word, is a very personal undertaking. Healers rarely talk about their work, despite its evident benefits to their clients. However, in a work of this scope, it is necessary to understand the healing process to some extent, to understand the healer.

The legendary Colin Bloy gets yet another mention at this point - and it is clear that Colin was not just an influence on the emerging worldview of the born-again Miller - he was an inspiration. Bloy's view was that healing was about rebalancing the energy of the earth, and through that, rebalancing the energies of the people, plants and places that were part of it. Healing was more than just putting things right; it was an embarkation on a sublime spiritual process.

How healing happens

There seem to be two broad schools of thought when it comes to healing.

One group uses the considerable power of the human consciousness to affect the much weaker power of the individual cells of the person, to bring about physical self-healing. Most of us are healing ourselves all the time, as part of the autonomic system (the one that keeps our heart beating and our breathing steady, without our having to pay any conscious attention to it). This system also organises the body at a cellular level, to sort out any routine ailments and imbalances. Only when the autonomic system cannot cope for some reason, does the healer come into play. Here the healer would direct the minute organisms, of which we are all composed, to deal with the problem. This process can be pretty effective when people are healing themselves, or when they are doing so under the instruction of a more experienced healer.

Taking this process one stage further, such conscious healing can also be used to help others by employing a form of telekinesis. In this mode, the power of the mind is harnessed to physically move minute objects, or to influence the activity of atoms and molecules at a distance. So, a healer could stimulate an increase in blood flow to an ailing organ, or encourage the activity of scavenging cells to remove infected or troublesome tissue. This type of healing is reasonably comprehensible to the open-minded lay person - and it only requires the current scientific paradigm to be severely bent for it to be brought into mainstream theory!

If you can get hold of them, the short books of retired admiral E H Shattock are an object lesson in how to describe this deceptively difficult subject in a down-to-earth, matter-of-fact manner.

The other method of healing, which is far more prevalent, doesn't use the input of the individual healer at all - indeed, the conscious practitioner is obliged to stand aside. In this method, the healer channels higher-level energy through themselves and into the patient - and/or removes unbalanced energy from the subject, through themselves, and out into the ground or the ether. The input side of the equation often involves the visualisation of white light being directed towards the individual being healed.

It is this latter process that is used by most people who are called 'healers' - and it is what Hamish employed when he effected a healing.

Healers come in all shapes and sizes, and with a bewildering array of techniques and a potential range of sources of their healing energy. As with dowsers, there seem to be almost as many methods as there are people deploying them. Few healers, however, can have had a more direct and earthy approach than the Bo'ness blacksmith.

> My feeling is that healing is a very private thing. People, who have a problem of any kind, need privacy. I don't talk about healing to anybody else. People are often very surprised that Ba and I have been doing healing for 20 years.
>
> Clients just ring us up and tell us they've got a problem. We go along and try to do something about it. We don't usually hear anything at all about the results of most healing sessions. However, maybe 2 or 3 years later, somebody else rings up and asks if we can help them. We ask where they got our name, and they tell us that someone we healed of a neck problem three years ago has been fine ever since. She's told them about us. I think it's the only way to do it - recommendation by word of mouth.
>
> We've done hundreds of houses. We do give healing to people who are not well, but we concentrate on people who are living in conditions that make them unwell.

For Hamish, his awareness of the ability of everyone to heal themselves and others started with his Near Death Experience. He became aware of the entities he terms The Management, whom he understood to be a delightful and compassionate group of beings that exist on a level a couple of evolutionary stages on from ourselves.

> They can see the bigger picture that we can't see, so I very much work through them. They can be contacted, using the earth's own energy, at any of the myriad of centres all over the earth. As we're all inter-connected parts of a vast energy network, to me healing is a very straightforward process.

> Ba and I don't diagnose, we merely act as the fuse in the plug - albeit a quite intentional fuse - to alleviate whatever problems our clients may have.

> Most of the problems we encounter seem to be emotional anomalies in their energy systems. All we try to do is to rebalance the energy system so that it sits more happily on the human frame.

> I used to do healing on my own, but it was pointed out that I could be sued by somebody who was not cured - or by somebody who was spaced out when they left a session and fell under a bus. I was astonished. It had never occurred to me that that could happen.

> The problem solved itself when Ba joined me here. We work together. She sits at the knees and the feet of the client and I stand behind them. Ba puts her hands on their feet and I hold the head. The mere act of doing that seems to release the flow of energy.

> We don't direct the energy flow; it goes automatically to those places that are out of balance. You leave it to the natural forces that you release - with the right intent - to rebalance the whole energetic structure.

> We use the same little energy centre every time. It's the strongest energy centre in the cottage. People sit in it and they relax totally. It's that relaxation, and the fact that two people are willing to spend an hour of their time, that helps

them to sort themselves out. The problem is that they are so relaxed they sometimes go to sleep. You have to be very patient. Part of the healing process is the time and the quiet and the balance.

That's how I heal. There's nothing very dramatic about it.

The wider landscape of healing

A lot of very good healers get into certain routines, which disturbs me. I came out of the National Federation (of Healers) partly because I didn't agree with the recommendation that you wear a white coat. It implies that you're doing something kind of po-faced - and it really is not like that. Also they have a technique of 'sculpting' the bad energy and throwing it away. That's not a good thing to do. If you're dealing with 'bad energy', the last thing you want to do is to scatter it about!

To me you're either a healer or you're not. I don't think there is a qualification that you can go through that can make you a healer. I think everybody can heal to some extent. The mother who picks up a child who has fallen down and gives them a cuddle is a healer. I define it as somebody who cares.

Because of the increasingly stringent social criteria relating to medical and social practices, there are now all sorts of ground rules you have to observe through political correctness - don't touch the client; you must have two of you there; you must record what you are doing; you must record what the results were, etc. To me, the healer is being forced to be more and more remote from the act of healing all the time. The act of healing is pure love, pure concern and the understanding of the stresses that somebody's going through - and trying to alleviate that in any way that you can. I think that's what the simple process of healing is all about.

Mike Colmer told me that as well as healing people, I should be healing the earth. At the time, I didn't know what he was talking about. However, once I came to realise that the earth's energy system is composed of millions of different frequencies, it started to become clearer. Although these frequencies are all completely natural vibrations of the planet, the human race finds some of them uncomfortable. you're not compatible with one of the frequencies that's passing through your kitchen, every time you cross it you'll compensate automatically, subconsciously - and in doing that you have to use your own energy.   If you use that little burst of energy 100 times a day and you don't know you're doing it, its pretty obvious that you'll start to feel tired and that life will get more difficult. In due course, you'll start to feel that your energy is depleting and you begin to feel ill.

To me, healing the earth is often more important than healing individuals, because at that point you can actually do something about the root causes of ill health.

I've seen it make a quite miraculous difference to people.

Healing, to someone who has only heard about it through the media, tends to have overtly religious connotations. Certainly, for those of a scriptural leaning, the energy can be sensed and described as coming directly, or indirectly, from their comprehension of the divine force or being. The obvious example of this being used in a public context is the practice of certain charismatic and evangelical ministers who can cause members of the congregation to crumple in a dazed heap in response to a gentle palm on the forehead. You can argue 'till the cows come home' about what is actually happening, but you can't deny it's extremely effective and routinely repeatable.

However, large numbers of healers see themselves as channelling or engaging with earth energy, or even cosmic energy. Increasingly, healers seem to be attributing their channelled power to something natural, something in the ether - which they would candidly accept is there for us all to use, all the time, if only we could remember how.

The approach that Hamish took could be said to bridge these two concepts. He was very straightforward about his relationship with The Management, which he saw as the source of the healing power he used.

I'm not asking and I'm not praying. Praying to me means the acceptance of subservience to some being. That's not the way I think it works - at least, that's not the way it works for me. The churches would like to think that healing only works by using a particular protocol, but I don't think it does.

151

Having said that, a ton of bricks might land on me now! (laughter) I feel it involves a natural energy that is flowing between every living being, which sometimes gets distorted or unbalanced.

I know that I can ask, on equal terms - I'm not genuflecting or begging. Once you've been up the tunnel and talked to these compassionate beings - they're just entities like us, on a different level. We're not subservient to them. I am in awe of their capacity to do things, but I have no trouble in yelling at them sometimes, when I think they've got it wrong! Although I have to accept that they have a wider overview and that they may have a perfectly good reason for not responding to my request for assistance. I have no feeling that I must act with humbleness and listen to them all the time. I am working on the same issues, even though I don't have access to the same level of knowledge. I have an understanding of how to deal with energy imbalances on this plane - more so than they have - but they have a much greater knowledge of how to deal with the manipulation of subtle energies. So, although we're in rather different fields of operation, essentially we're all trying to achieve much the same thing.

Hamish and Ba, together with most people following the protocol espoused by Colin Bloy, were actually healing the earth most of the time - and improving the lot of people affected by energy imbalances almost as a by-product of that process.

One of the fundamental tenets of the work of Colin's Fountain Group was that if a number of minds could be focused or channels opened, this would have far more benefit than just one healer working alone. Whether you can apply the basics of fluid dynamics to the flow of healing energy I rather doubt, but it does seem intuitively sound that a larger group of minds working positively in a population will have more effect than just a few.

There has been much discussion about just how big a proportion of a society is necessary to nudge a community away from a path of self-destruction towards a more positive outlook. Hamish was in no doubt about the benefits of group action, and it was one of the driving forces behind his establishment of the Parallel Community, which we will discuss later.

> There are those who pooh-pooh some of these organised Peace Days - but once you get 5,000 or 6,000 minds focused on one thing, I'm certain it does have a powerful effect.

Hamish may have been following and expanding upon the healing path opened up by Colin, but he was not alone in realising that the healing of individuals is just the tip of the iceberg. One could argue that personal healing is just one more method of effecting a temporary respite from pain, albeit a dramatically less intrusive one - and could even be likened to the taking of aspirin to relieve a headache. It may give some welcome relief, but unless the root cause of the imbalance is sorted out, the expression of the illness will just resurface somewhere else. In this context, it is relevant again to refer to the groundbreaking work of HM's dowsing contemporary, Billy Gawn.

Over recent decades, Billy has carried out very detailed research around his home in Northern Ireland - a realm haunted by troublesome imbalances for many centuries. He has studied the impact of stone circles and chambered tombs, including those he has erected himself, on the health of the energetic framework of the area. The results are little short of a revelation.

If Billy's work is borne out by future researchers, then the whole nature of the spiritual, the mental and even the physical health of great tracts of our planet will need to be completely rethought.

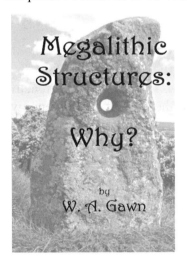

Megalithic Structures: Why?

by
W. A. Gawn

He has shown, by dowsing, that the 'correct' location of stones and other objects on specific energy lines can have a direct, beneficial impact on the quality of earth energy in the surrounding network. I'm not talking here about just the energy in your bedroom, or even on your allotment - but energy patterns over a considerable swathe of the countryside.

While Billy's approach emphasises physical location, and Hamish majored more on intent, the practical outcomes point to the same virtuous spiral - reduced detrimental energy in the land leading to a more harmonious balance of

the etheric network, leading to a more contented population, leading to
improved individual and corporate health, leading to a reduced level of
stress in society, leading to reduced detrimental energy in the land,
leading to . . .

I can almost feel Colin Bloy, nodding vigorously from the otherworld.

Healing in style

Many styles of healing rely on ceremony - or at least incorporate some
measure of it. In certain circumstances, it can clearly provide a
framework on which to mount a healing event, while in others it can even
be quite theatrical. Hamish was, typically, rather dismissive of the need
for such approaches.

> I've done work on houses in the London area where the
> residents have employed flamboyant practitioners - people
> who sacrifice dolls and burn this and that. They seem to be
> happy to pay enormous sums of money for somebody who
> prances about theatrically, presumably because they are
> desperate and want to see something happening. Sadly,
> there are charlatans in every walk of life.
>
> When I do healing, there's nothing much they can see - and
> consequently some of these people are a bit disappointed.
>
> In the established churches, ceremony has taken the place
> of the real issues of religion. The various denominations feel
> that without the ceremony, nobody would believe. If they
> didn't have the big pointed hat, the funny curly stick and gold
> robes, they clearly feel that they wouldn't be important
> enough for people to turn up and listen to them. To some
> extent, they are probably right - let's face it; most of their
> ceremonies are incredibly boring!
>
> I do understand that a lot of people are looking for something
> beyond the norm that they can believe in. It's just that my
> 'beyond the norm' is blissfully without attachments; without
> material bits and pieces, and certainly without any funny 'ats
> - it's all very natural. I feel that there is such incredible
> dignity in natural things. They don't need any dressing up.
> In fairness, I don't mind people using ceremony, if that

means something to them or helps them along the way, but I'm not at all comfortable about being part of it.

While some people are on a colossal ego trip, most healers are coming from the right place. They just want to help. They are aware of the problems and they are doing everything they can to assist, in their own particular way. We all use different methods, but basically we are all doing exactly the same thing.

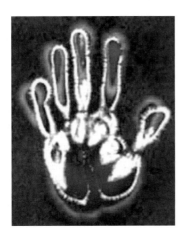

When I'm healing the earth, I'm just trying to make happily balanced energies available to anyone who has something wrong, rectifying anomalies in the bio-magnetic field.

With people and animals, applying energy is a bit like doing some remote sculpting, if you like. You can actually use your fingers to guide the energy. When people take photographs using Kirlian photography, you can see these little straw-coloured bits coming out of the

Kirlian photograph of energy emanating from a human hand

end of your fingers. You can use those to put energy into other bodies, to work with it like a sculptor would clay.

Why is there a need for healing?

For a layman like myself, and probably for many of you reading this book, an obvious question that arises in relation to the healing process is that if The Management are so much more advanced than us and allegedly ethically pure, why don't 'they' just get on and sort out the subtle imbalances that give rise to ill-health and discomfort in the first place, without the prompting of lower-order creatures like ourselves?

In a sense, it is the secular parallel to the debate in religious circles about the prevalence of the all-seeing, all-knowing and all-loving deity, amidst a planet riven with hatred, disease and general unpleasantness. Many of the answers put forward to this question by theologians and philosophers of a religious bent are, at best, unconvincing to the post-modern mind.

Even given that we are trying to explain the inexplicable, the most workable scenario that has been proffered to date is that we are being put through some form of individual and/or corporate trial to establish if we are suitable to enter the Golden Kingdom. While the idea of a real-life Matrix has an uncomfortably credible feel to it, it raises so many more questions than answers.

The more acceptable response, at least in the western tradition, is that we don't know yet and all will be revealed at some point in the future. You can't really argue with that line of reasoning, but it doesn't give you much of a pointer as to how to make the best of this cycle, back in the here and now.

Hamish Miller was attracted to the school of healing that holds the view that The Management are not all-powerful in this dimension - and, although 'they' have a level of understanding and the ability to act at a higher level, 'they' are unable to interfere directly in the everyday affairs of planet earth.

If healers seek advice, and are able to open a portal of enlightenment, then there is the opportunity to gently influence the physical world at the subtlest of levels. The body in question heals itself, but uses the power of information and guidance from a higher level. In that scenario, the healer is, almost literally and to quote Hamish's own description, 'the fuse in the plug' - allowing the unmeterably tiny flow of esoteric energy to revitalise the patient.

This would put the relationship between the healer, the client and The Management on a much more even footing. Each would operate in their own sphere and each would play their own part in the healing process. This relationship between man and Management is one to which we will need to return later on.

Another question that may well have occurred to anyone considering the nature of the healing process is why an intermediary is needed at all. If, as Hamish stated, we are all healers at some basic level, why don't we just sit quietly, pick up the psychic phone to The Management and sort ourselves out? Doubtless there are the gifted few who can do just that. However, with both healing and dowsing, it can often be difficult to separate yourself sufficiently from the task in hand for it to work effectively. As Hamish himself said 'You can't do it properly with a foot in both camps'. If you are the recipient, it is much easier to have a healer to act as your channel.

On a personal level, I will happily help others to at least identify the presence of potentially detrimental energies in their homes. Yet, when things were going palpably wrong in our own house - and despite a couple of decades of practice at sensing the same energies - I could find nothing untoward. We were obliged to call in our friend, the professional dowser Alan Neal, who was able to find the offending strands and deal with them.

As we talked through this important issue, I was aware that across the table was a vastly experienced eighty-something year old healer, with his left arm nestled in a makeshift sling, held together with a safety pin. HM had fallen up a flight of granite steps and, despite the air of joviality about such a minor mishap, clearly he had been in considerable pain at the time. However, friends had called in the evening before we met to provide him with a flow of healing energy and he was patently feeling much more comfortable, or at least more optimistic, as a result of their input.

Why aren't healers wealthy?

On my first dowsing course, I was told that you couldn't make yourself rich by dowsing. If you do attempt it, for example by trying to divine lottery numbers, then the results you will get are meaningless. Worse still, the natural ability that you've rediscovered can desert you. There is a certain internal logic to this, in that the desire for excessive wealth is clearly one of the social cul-de-sacs that our post-modern civilisation has driven into, and any inner wisdom would not add fuel to that particular fire. However, experience indicates that there seems to be no intrinsic harm in making a modest charge for helping others by using your intuition. Only those with a fortunate inheritance, a good pension or the single-mindedness of a monk could afford to do good works all day instead of earning a crust. For some, it would appear that the way to resolve this ethical dilemma is to turn the question back on itself - to dowse for a reasonable rate of return (although, given the intrinsic benefit to the practitioner, I would suggest you ask a friend to do this for you!).

The ever-pragmatic Miller worked through this particular monetary minefield is his own inimitable way:

> I feel I would like to be able to do all my healing activities for nothing. But I can't, because to go healing I've got to come out of the forge, and then I lose the productive time that I

could be working there. Even at my age, I still need to work to keep active and to keep my head above water.

Matthew Manning (and I'm not comparing myself to him) is one of the greatest healers in the country. He had an immense problem, because he had a reputation as a successful healer of cases that the doctors left behind. He got to the stage where, with the best will in the world, he could try to heal about 60 people a week, but he had over 300 people a week asking to be healed. He felt he was being asked to play god, and it was really disturbing him that he had to turn away the other 240.

So, he decided to start doing healing events in a theatre, to try to reach more people. What he then found was that people started to criticise him, because he had this enormous talent - and he was charging a fee for it! His response was that if he didn't charge for it, he would have to earn a living another way, which would reduce his capacity as a healer even further. It was a terrible dichotomy for him. He even took on some staff healers that he had selected himself - but the clients didn't want his assistants, they wanted him personally.

I find it legitimate that I charge when I have to come out of the workshop. I try to get my petrol money back, but I do find it difficult to charge a sensible rate. Mind you, I find it difficult to charge for the blacksmithing too - because I just like doing it!

There are many healers who only ask for contributions, which is one way of dealing with it.

Even if levying a charge is an acceptable and necessary process for most healers, in an increasingly hard-line capitalist society, how do you go about setting a reasonable fee?

If a healer is really competent and cures you of something that is mindblowingly depleting, then £1,000 is nothing - yet £20 can be too much. It's beyond monetary value.

One of the easiest ways is to look out of the window and if there's a big new car outside . . . (laughter), I have no difficulty then in charging £50. At the end of the day, it depends entirely on who they are and how much distress they are in.

I was almost in tears with an elderly lady in Penzance not long ago, who was close to death. She asked me 'How much do you charge?' and I could only reply 'nothing' - so she asked 'Can I give you a bar of chocolate?' It was lovely - richly rewarding. The reward is in knowing that people may have a better chance of getting well.

Most of us would be willing to 'help an old lady across the road', but equally most of us might think twice about doing the same for a rough-looking bloke carrying a gun. How did Hamish the healer evaluate the people who came to him for help?

It doesn't register at all. To me, they are just another sick being. Their rhythms are out of kilter, so you try to put them right. You know you can't sort their problems out, but you can give them the strength to help them to do it themselves. Many of the people who seek healing from us have such low self-esteem and such low self-confidence. If you can just give them the energy to cope with the next couple of days, you feel you're doing something valuable - but you don't know exactly what it is.

Adventures with animals

Knowing that most healers are called in to deal with people's pets and domestic animals almost as often as their family members, I was interested to know what experience Hamish had of healing the nation's fauna.

I've carried out healing for dogs, mostly.

I don't have such an affinity with cats, because they can have something like 37 varieties of flea, of which 20-odd are known to bite human beings. I know this obscure fact because, when I had the farmhouse in Sussex, I had a terrible skin problem. It was so bad, that I went up to St Bartholomew's Hospital in London. They told me that, as I was living in a farmhouse, it was almost certainly one of the animals. To find out which one it was, I was to take a sheet of brown paper and comb the fleas out of whatever pets I had. Barts would then analyse the results and let me know which one it was. I told them that we had two horses, two donkeys, ducks, two cats, gerbils and various other creatures. The specialist looked at me over his spectacles and said 'Move!' Actually, they were very helpful, but I mean, how could I put a donkey on a bit of paper? (laughter) Anyway, as it happened, shortly afterwards, our big grey cat died - and my skin irritation went away completely. I've never got very close to cats since!

Animals respond to what you are doing, but clearly they don't know what 'you are up to', especially as you are not actually touching them - and obviously you can't tell them what is supposed to happen.

I am impressed with the work of Dr. Vav Simon, who is an animal chiropractor on the Isle of Wight. She has carried out healing experiments using a piece of electronic equipment designed by Harry Oldfield. Harry's machine projects a graphical display showing an aura (the energetic body which surrounds the physical one) on to a screen so that it can be seen by a large audience.

On one occasion, Vav was doing a demonstration of healing and chiropractic work with horses, to a big group of veterinary surgeons. As you can imagine, these are highly suspect procedures from a professional vet's point of view. A horse that she hadn't seen before was brought in. The horse didn't know what was going on, obviously - and had nothing to say about it. The screen above her showed its aura. You could see the effect of her hands on the horse's aura showing up in red on the screen - and you could see the difference in the aura of the horse as she moved up and down. She said that some of the vets were almost in tears, because they could see this horse reacting to her healing - which they didn't believe in. You can't cook that sort of thing on the stage, because the horse doesn't know how to cheat! (laughter) It just reacts naturally. It was a hugely important experiment.

It helps to confirm my faith in healing as an effective process - and I feel that much the same is happening when I treat people. They don't know exactly what you're doing, but they are still reacting to it

Trying to use the current tools to gauge the effects of healing is a bit like poking a dentist's drill into the North Sea to see if you can find any oil. We know that there are some very meaningful things happening when we heal, but we haven't got the tools to measure them at the moment.

...and with flora

Many years ago, I read Lyall Watson's book 'Supernature'. He was researching the energetic reaction of plants to various stimuli. The experiment that particularly impressed me was the way that the auras of plants reacted if you threatened to burn one of their leaves with a cigarette. Using an earlier form of Kirlian photography, they were shown to recoil, presumably in fear. I felt that was fascinating.

When I started working with the auras of trees and plants myself, I found some fascinating things. There are some huge trees with practically no aura at all, but there are some tiny trees with huge, energetic auras. I didn't quite know why this should be. For me, this was part of the build up to the realisation that we are connected to everything - physically, metaphysically, and cosmically. We are all One. Eventually, I came to appreciate that we humans are composed of bunches of energy; that trees are made up of bunches of energy and that plants and rocks are also bunches of energy. We are all composed of much the same stuff.

We've planted about 1,500 trees in Cornwall and I've asked almost every one of them if they wanted to be planted where I was about to bed them in. It was a two-way communication. It's not just about sensing the aura of the trees; it's the recognition that they are living beings - and treating them accordingly. I've lost count of the number of times I've put a sapling on a potential planting place and dowsed 'Do you want to grow here?' - only to get back a thunderous 'NO'. You have to respect that, because it knows, I think, whether the roots will go down into something beneficial or something detrimental - but you wouldn't know for sure until you'd dug a hole.

Individual planting conditions vary enormously. I don't think you can just work out where the energy lines go and plant a row of trees, because some of the trees won't like that particular type of energy. They're a bit like people; there are areas where they feel comfortable and places where they feel uncomfortable. I can live with that.

Inevitably, if I decide to plant a tree in a particular spot, perhaps because it marks the turn of a path or some other cosmetic feature, I usually find there's a huge great granite boulder right beneath the chosen location. If the tree says 'I don't want to be here', as often as not you can actually stick a rod in the ground and find the boulder - so I'm convinced that they know best! Over the years, we've planted about 1500 trees and we've lost about 300 to rabbits, wind and drought, which I reckon is a pretty reasonable score.

Community Spirits

There can be few people who have taken dowsing beyond the initial stage of finding that they can get rods to move in response to a question, who have not then gone on to consider other aspects of the non-physical continuum.

Beings without bodies

Many, many people who have never even heard of dowsing have the feeling that what are usually termed spirits, souls or entities play some ill-defined part in the wider world around us. Some of those people may have had a background of one or other of the major world religions, where the non-physical world gets a copious mention, but not much of a digestible explanation. Meanwhile others, who may have no formal scriptural upbringing, are nonetheless aware of phenomena beyond everyday understanding, which has a genuine reality for them.

At a wider level again, just about everyone has heard a good ghost story that has, quite literally, spooked them. Children are particularly vulnerable to being frightened by such ideas, perhaps because they have yet to erect a seemingly solid scientific wall around their reality. They have yet to fully separate the well-documented and the laboratory-tested environment from the uncomfortable, but often all-too-real, wilderness beyond it.

Science has edged the wall of the city of certainty out into the wildwood of mystery, but in many ways the wildwood still seems as large and as dense as ever. Each new discovery, each new piece of the jigsaw, poses another set of questions, and exposes other new fields for potential exploration. I feel that we can be justifiably proud that, in the last century in particular, we have come to know a great deal about the planet of which we are custodians - but equally we must be very humble in the realisation that we actually understand very little.

Spirit levels

If you thought that the NDE was a good example of things we have only just started to take seriously, here's another. Spirits exist.

Even a journeyman improver, like myself, can come across a spirit. I am not sensitive enough to bump into them in the street, as some of the more clairvoyant of dowsers can - and I'm not too sorry about this minor impairment! However, when I am out on a site, especially a sacred site or the scene of an accident or a battle - and if I ask the right question in the right way, I can often be led to a disembodied bundle of energy that used to be a person. On a good day, I can ascertain a little about them, but I always leave anything further to those with more experience and sensitivity.

The first time this happened to me was when I was on a weekend course in Tavistock in Devon. One of our group commented that a particular part of the parish church, to one side of the altar, seemed unusually cold on what passes for a warm day in these parts. The tutor came over to investigate and pronounced it to be an entity - and that it was starting to move in response to our taking an interest. Most of us shuffled with undue haste down the aisle towards the door. By the time our leader was saying 'Come back, come back, this is really interesting!' we were already heading out into the reassurance of the afternoon sunshine. Sometimes dowsing can lead you into whole areas of research that you thought were just fairy stories - and of course, some of them are indeed just that.

Getting to grips with spirits does require some insight and some experience, but I am assured it is conceptually no more difficult than a car driver learning to drive a bus. There is a growing consensus amongst those who talk about the spirit world as an everyday experience that most of the ghosts, ghouls and things-that-go-bump-in-the-night are nothing more than people who don't realise that they have died. It took Hamish a little while to understand that he had left his body, potentially for good, and with a little direction found his way up the tunnel. People who die suddenly in accidents or murders have no time to make the mental adjustment. For those of us brought up in an educational peer group whose members assumed that death is the end, I am sure it is a bit confusing to put it mildly, to find yourself still here. It's enough to make you scream and shout and to try to attract someone's attention to the fact that you're floating about when you should be . . . . well, you shouldn't be.

A whole new area of work has opened up for those of a sensitive nature in helping these lost souls to move on. Some of those left behind seem quite comfortable with their unexpected lot, sat quietly in a churchyard or walking through their favourite garden - even though it might now be a dual carriageway. Others are anything but - desperately trying to make their presence known, by any means at their disposal, in a world they can sense, but can't contact directly.

Hamish on the healing journey

To Hamish, following his NDE, all this became pretty apparent, and not at all frightening.

> When I first had the forge at Nut Lane, I met Trevor Nevins, who was an extraordinary person. He was a Yorkshireman with a huge capacity for looking through the portals, but he was trapped in a very difficult body that made it difficult for him to walk. Trevor was very aware of earth energies, earth spirits and trapped beings - and I worked with him, and his wife Sheila, for maybe six months, off and on. He taught me about entities - how they behaved, what they did, what you could do to help them. Basically, they are quite simply energy bodies. Ninety eight per cent of them were incredibly lonely, just desperately trying to say "I'm here". Some would move something, like a poltergeist. Others would create a smell, or appear in peripheral vision.
>
> It was Trevor that taught me, over many months, that they are only people like us - at a slightly different level. So many of them are really incredibly lonely, and they need our help to move on. The work Trevor and I did with them developed until I got going on my own. To me, they are always fascinating balls of energy, with a separate existence, but without a physical manifestation. I became aware of the need to check if there could be one present, to dowse for the direction of it, and then go towards it with love, rather than fear. Nearly all of the time, they are met with fear and, needless to say, that does nothing to help them.

Sheila and Trevor Nevins

You can actually dowse them quite easily and you can feel them - they have their own aura. As soon as you can do that, they realise that you know they're there, and you can start a form of communication. The dowser can't decide whether an entity should be released or not, because you don't know the wider picture, so once again I consult The Management. However, in the vast majority of cases The Management agree that they should move on - and whoooosh they're off - sometimes without even saying goodbye! (laughter)

I have occasionally come across people, who have been 'possessed' by spirits that have been afraid to move on, and who have latched themselves on to a being. A lot of them have just one objective - and that's to survive. One way of doing that, at least in the short term, is to get into a symbiotic relationship with somebody who is still living. That way, they have a body of sorts, even though there is somebody else in there with them - which, of course, makes it a bit complicated for all of us. Once they've developed that symbiotic relationship, they take their energy from the living person, and they can continue to exist in that particular way as long as the host doesn't crack up. The spirit has a reasonably comfortable place to be, within this body, and they can be extremely difficult to move on! I had one lady screaming that she wanted rid of this thing, but she was afraid … afraid of what would happen to it, because it had developed into something of a love-hate relationship. She was afraid that it might have been an unborn baby.

I have no fear of spirits or different levels of beings. I'm extremely lucky in that respect, and I couldn't have taken on this type of work, but for the NDE. Had I not had that special insight, I might have had an inherent fear of the spirit world that I couldn't cope with. However, I don't have that fear now, and strangely enough the spirits realise it. In a way, it's a bit like people who are able to deal with aggressive dogs.

The view of 'souls' that leave their temporary residence at the end of a cycle, but by some dint of lack of understanding of the opportunities, or the lack of revelatory guidance, fail to gain enough impetus to move on, was all part of Hamish's view of the wider hierarchy and continuum of existence.

There are correlations here with the concept of karma, which is so fundamental to the eastern philosophies. This is the idea that the energy that has accumulated and developed within an entity is constantly changing, but that this is only really apparent in the period between the end of one cycle and the start of the next. Essentially, you are what you are when it's time to move on. If you have acquired sufficient wisdom (traditionally called 'merit' in the east-west translation) by that point, maybe you get the option to evolve further, with or without the aid of an aluminium tunnel. If not, then the trajectory of release is too feeble, and eventually you fall back into the material world. In this case, you may eventually have the extreme good fortune or emerging wisdom to merge with the matter of a forthcoming being, and that could open another possible stairway to the next stage.

The Power of the Circle

Guarded from view behind a protective swathe of Hamish's beloved Treviscoe trees is a magical place that starts to show how he was using his own resources to move on from his theoretical discoveries.

The stone circle and its accompanying artefacts are part spiritual retreat, part Cornish sculpture garden and part outdoor dowsing laboratory. This was Hamish working with the world around him - and drawing others generously into the fold.

> It was always a very special field for me, because it always <u>felt</u> very good. There's a pouring down of energy from Trencrom Hill and an energy line going through it. However, I felt I needed to do something more with the field; there was so much more potential; I wanted to mark it in some way. There was a little energy centre right in the middle of the field, which had 20 radials - quite strong for such a small source.

> One day, a man called Ted Seaton arrived to show me a stone, carved with a head, which seemed to be of Celtic origin. It certainly had some unusual energy attached to it. When I placed it in the middle of the energy centre in the house, it produced a series of remarkable, dowsable energy manifestations. This started me off investigating the impact of placing different objects and designs in the middle of energy centres, such as the one in our field.

The Seed of Life at Treviscoe

Around 2004 or 2005, Ted introduced me to an amazing lady from Wales called Diana Rhodes. She's a tiny, wheelchair-bound person, but she's incredibly energetic and dynamic - the sort that doesn't take no for an answer.

She asked us if we would join a 'gathering of indigenous peoples' in Wales, where she was going to inaugurate a Seed of Life design, cut into the ground, as a focus for peace for spiritual people from around the world. However, we couldn't go to the event, because we were committed elsewhere. Diana replied to our apology for absence by saying that if we couldn't go to her event, we would have to build our own Seed of Life in Cornwall. So, that's where the original idea for the design came from.

After a bit of thought, we hit upon the idea of cutting the Seed of Life design around the energy centre in the field - and then putting a stone circle around it.

I felt I wanted to mark the centre and the four cardinal directions with larger stones, so that I could start locating it in space and time, and so that I could start working with it. I then intended to mark each of the radials with a small stone, which is what I felt the ancient people used to do in years gone by.

We marked it out very accurately in paint, ready for cutting. Ba suggested that some of her friends might be wiling to help us and, in due course, an appropriate day was arranged to cut the first turf. The group made a start with trowels and other domestic garden implements - and it rapidly became apparent that the process would take many months at that pace. Luckily, another lady arrived to help who was a farmer's wife. She came prepared with a proper spade, and things started to happen with a bit more gusto. After a while, she went off to get another friend, who turned out to be a local gravedigger - so in the end the digging part of the job was completed in a few hours.

In our naivety, we decided to mark out the cut design from the rest of the field by planting the earthen sections with wild flower plants and seeds. What we had overlooked, was that we have about 400 million rabbits, who watched this lunch being presented with some enthusiasm, and promptly ate the lot! It clearly needed to be marked up with something more robust, so we asked everyone who came to the site to bring a white stone. Now it's an amalgam of stones from all over the country and all over the world. There are stones from Australia, America, Europe - and it just adds to the energy of the place. In fact, it's become so well known that now you can pick it up on Google.

So far, so good, but I was still keen to erect my stone circle. In yet another startling piece of synchronicity, I was asked by some friends, Michael and Marianne Brookman, to find a home for a 'collection' of Mendip limestone rocks. I had given them some help on energy matters on a couple of occasions, and I was aware that they had amassed a quantity of these large stones, effectively as garden artefacts. They had moved these stones from one house to another, but then they decided to emigrate to Spain - and clearly they couldn't take the sandstone rocks with them. So, they called to ask if I had a use for them. I asked him how many they had and, to my surprise, Michael replied that they had 24. I immediately realized that this meant I could use one for each radial and one for each of the cardinal points. Just the job. Within a fortnight, the rocks had been delivered on a lorry.

The stone circle at Treviscoe - 2010

With so much else going on in my life at the time, they lay where they landed for a couple of years, waiting to be erected. From time to time I tried to deal with them myself, using a wheelbarrow, but they were just too big and too heavy.

I got around to marking out the radials (that's the basic radials that are always at a place at rest) with wooden pegs, but the stones themselves carried on lounging expectantly.

Eventually, I had to admit defeat and I hired a local man, who arrived with the most clapped-out digger you have ever seen. Needless to say, he thought I was quite mad, but it was a job . . . However, as the project progressed, he really got into the task in hand and soon he had the holes dug and the stones in position.

Initially, the stones did nothing at all. I was rather disappointed and I even wondered if I'd done the wrong thing by erecting them. They just sat there; they'd never been in a circle before and it took some time, over three months in fact, for anything to start happening between them. Then, one lovely evening, I was dowsing around them and I realized that there was energy passing between them - they were sending out their own radials and communicating as a group. They've been at it for some years now, but I've still got no idea what they are saying (laughter).

During the 1999 total solar eclipse, a totally new east-west earth energy was drawn into the circle, forming the powerful spiral that you can dowse today. Interestingly, that energy line has stayed in place, even though the sandstone rocks that define the energy centre are not the typical Menhirs of the Cornish landscape, whose function might be partly to pin the serpentine energy lines to a chosen spot.

It now has energy manifestations at the centre (which we have discussed earlier in this book), which are changing all the time. The first indication was a simple cruciform shape, almost like a Celtic cross, in the centre of the circle. It started as quite a small icon, but grew to the outer limits of the circle. Over time, it morphed into a lemniscates (the ancient Greek symbol for infinity). In the winter of 2009/10, it developed into three intertwined lemniscates - forming, what looked like, a six-petalled flower.

I feel this development is being assisted by the fact that we use the circle to celebrate the Celtic calendar. Every six weeks we have a ceremony to mark the passing of the year - and we celebrate the solstices in particular. Sometimes there are just two or three people present; at other times we have a more elaborate spiritual procedure, with an assembled multitude. As I have said earlier, I'm not all that keen in being involved in ceremonies, but I can't deny that the regular gathering of many consciousnesses at this site is having a profound effect on the quality of the energy in the circle. Although they are very simple ceremonies, the circle seems to be reacting to the hundreds of consciousnesses that are interacting with it over time. The essence of the ceremonies is to tune into the energy of the earth. That's why I think it's starting to acknowledge the participants and to 'communicate' by means of manifestations. Mind you, I don't know where it's going to go to from here.

Personally, I feel I don't need the ceremony as such, as I can tune in straight away. I'm very familiar with the energy and how it changes. I'm sure that applies to many of the people who come here regularly. However, there are always a few strangers, new people, for whom the ceremony may help to give a certain amount of structure and focus. Sometimes there are people who join in, but can't make much sense of it; don't get much out of the process - but even they seem to enjoy the experience, albeit for some reason that they can't analyse.

I am quite certain that there is a deliberate communication from and to both people and place. I also feel that there is more communication, clearer communication, when larger numbers of people are involved.

As time has passed, the basic 20 radials, which are still in place (they haven't moved at all), have been augmented by smaller radial lines either side of the primary line. So, between each stone there are usually two extra lines. However, this is not always consistent, and occasionally I can find three radial lines or just one line between the stones. It seems to be work in progress! I firmly believe that it's the circle that's becoming more demonstrative, rather than me becoming more sensitive.

The stones we have erected are marking both the radial energy of the place and the energetic boundary of what has now become a 'consecrated' sacred space.

The siting of this sacred space presents something of a conundrum to any dowser who has not been involved with the Treviscoe arrangement. Hamish stated that he dowsed for the most powerful energy centre on his land, where he could erect a future stone circle. He further confirmed that at the outset, there was just one energy line coming down from Trencrom Hill, which passed through the spot to which he was directed. However, he is certain that the 20 radials and an initial spiral were already in place. It would seem unlikely given the available time and the experience of the dowser that he just 'missed' a second earth energy line. Equally, I have never come across an energy spiral without at least two intersecting lines. The initial radials may have been the remanance of some previous structure, but again Hamish didn't detect one.

If dowsing challenges some of the accepted laws of physics, then Hamish's stone circle site challenges some of the accepted laws of dowsing. How very apt!

It even leads us into the intriguing area of awareness independent of time. If Hamish was asking for the best place for his forthcoming sacred space, could it be that he was led to a site that would become appropriate as a result of the moving of the second line during the physical and energetic changes brought about by the eclipse?

When you think about it that way, it could make sense.

Time for a cup of tea - or something stronger!

There are already several works of art around the site and in due course I would like to put a significant sculpture in the middle of it. We already have one of the sculptures, which will describe the four basic elements.

The one representing Air is in place, with bits of a plough that blow in the wind and make a sound like a monastery bell. I would like the Water feature to be one of those sculptures where water circulates through the sculpted form. The Fire sculpture will need to have some active flames in it. I haven't quite worked out the one representing Earth yet, but I intend to make these this year!!

Pause for silent contemplation.

Part Three

The Afterglow

The Parallel Community

The imperative for change

Almost without exception, people who have been through an NDE come back with their lives changed - usually quite radically, and usually with a very much more positive outlook.

For Hamish, it opened up new and unimagined areas of thought and research, and led to him taking the further life-changing leap into the world of the dowser. This, in turn, brought him into contact with like-minded people from across the globe.

You don't have to go through a trauma of the Miller magnitude to understand that all is not well in the world around us. Environmental degradation, amoral social and commercial structures, increasing stress and declining satisfaction, climatic instability . . . Yet, I would not contend that everything in the world is going wrong. Indeed it's part of my personal philosophy that in the longer term, everything comes back into balance, physically and non-physically - but, of course, we may not, as a species, be part of that longer term.

For those who have had the 'benefit' of an NDE, the call to action seems to be well nigh universal. Only their actions tend to differ, dependent on the culture of the individual and the make up of their residual baggage. For Hamish, the first and most obvious personal change was to move away from the world of industry and commerce. The second was to move towards an alternative that would make sense of his new-found realisation that the material and the metaphysical worlds were equally important and inextricably mixed.

As we have seen, his personal journey took him around the world, several times, and into realms that he would not have even considered topics for rational conversation just a few years earlier. The appreciation that his personal journey was just one pixel in the vast screen of planetary life, drove him ever onward to seek some form of action that could make a positive impact on the widest picture.

> The final trigger was the life-changing experience I had at Castle Hill in New Zealand. Just prior to that, I had another extraordinary hospital experience, in Australia, where I nearly passed over due to a serious and unexplained illness - and

that led me to being there. It was one of the first times that I'd been given a clear vision of something that I couldn't physically see. I was aware for four consecutive nights of these huge beings - and I mean massive - behind my hospital bed with deep, deep, voices. They were not particularly happy about having to look after (laughter) this creature, because from their perspective I was made of very poor material! I had a very clear idea from somewhere of what they might look like, so I did a sketch on the day that I left the hospital. I can't tell you what a mind-blowing experience it was, when I went into a meditation at Castle Hill at the centre of the marai, the source of all the Waitaha activity in that sacred place.

It was a beautiful dawn. Ba was sitting at the side of the marai and, as I sat there in the centre, I became aware of being watched.

I resisted it for a long time, but eventually I had to turn round – and I saw two massive great stone beings behind me. I shuddered all over with a powerful feeling of anticipation that something important was going to happen.

TWO IMMENSE 'BEINGS' SKETCHED
WHILE IN AUSTRALIAN HOSPITAL.

Seeing these two great creatures there, recognising them as the two beings I had sketched in the hospital and understanding why they'd said I was made of such poor material was a cathartic experience.

They were made four million years ago of Limestone, which is composed of the shells and skeletons of trillions of little creatures that once had a physical life - and somehow that life force is still in the rock. It was then that I became aware of the ultra-bass voice coming through.

What possibly isn't in the book (In Search of the Southern Serpent) deeply enough is the <u>pain</u> these elders were expressing in trying to come to terms with what we had done to the earth in the last 2000 years - and what had happened to the human species during that time. To them, it seemed we were in a process of absolute moral deterioration. They seemed to understand that our financial system is integral to the promotion of the sale of munitions; that there is a need to create war to keep the armaments factories in business . . . They didn't have access to appropriate language to get their message across, but they were very, very anxious that I understood their distress. They weren't complaining, but there was a desperate concern that we needed to do something immediately. For me, it was a traumatic moment. When we left Castle Hill, I knew I was at the end of that phase of my development. Everything I had experienced in my post NDE life had led up to that point - but something had to evolve from there, and I had to take responsibility for the insight I had been given.

Philosophy into practice

But how can any person, even one given the sacred spark of enlightenment, make any progress against the scale and belligerence of the greedy and bellicose forces that are moving the species ever further from the source of reconciliation. Some of us would reduce our impact by attempting to live a life of constructive contemplation. Some would rail privately and be consumed by a fire of frustration and fury. Hamish, ever the practical and determined Scot, decided to start a quiet revolution.

In 'It's Not Too Late', which was written in 1998, I was fulminating about all the things that the elders I had contacted in New Zealand were worried about. Ba and I talked about writing another book, but she felt that wasn't the right thing to do, because we would just reach the same people who had read the last one. We would have been preaching to the converted. Somehow or other, we had to get in touch with a wider, younger audience.

The Parallel Community started around our kitchen table. The message I wanted to get out was so urgent, yet I had no idea of how to start. Five of us got together and my friend,

Gary Merrill, said, from absolutely nowhere, 'Everybody, every human being, deserves to live in peace - but we'll never have that peace until we claim the right'. It was one of those seminal moments. I felt a tingle down the spine. It was the moment the Parallel Community was born.

The idea of claiming the right to live in peace became a reality. It began to have some sort of form. A week or so later, half a dozen of us met up and somebody said 'We're not going to fight them on their own ground. We're going to be working in parallel. So why don't we call ourselves the Parallel Community?'

We realised we would need to have a very simple, easily recognisable logo. The lemniscates was a pictogram that I had dowsed at earth energy centres in New Zealand. It seemed very appropriate, as it is a representation of infinity. It represents an equal balance of male and female energy; infinite power at its centre with perfect balance and it is one of the most recognisable of the ancient symbols - so we adopted it.

A few months later, we decided to launch the Parallel Community at a public meeting. The public meeting is on record. It was wonderful, because this was a wet November night in Penzance and over 170 people turned up at the Queens Hotel on the seafront - when we were only expecting about 20! We had very rashly offered them a free glass of wine for their contribution, but it soon ran out!

People turned up from all over the place and they were very, very enthusiastic about the whole idea. We tried to explain what we were going to do, but that was difficult, because we ourselves hadn't formulated exactly what we wanted the PC to do at that stage. We wanted to leave it to the people who joined to come in with their ideas and to make it evolve.

We started off with the idea of communicating with the Transition Towns movement, which had been started to encourage the building up of local communities and to foster local independence. From that enthusiastic, but humble beginning, it has gradually grown into an international network.

After the first meeting, we sent out a newsletter and started getting feedback about local problems. We did a number of talks around the country, which were always well received. We had a combined meeting with the Steiner School and Transition Totnes, with 150 people turning up, who were all very enthusiastic. Everywhere we went people were very supportive. We may not have been very organised, but we had certainly struck a rich vein. People, lots of people, wanted a different kind of society.

The thing that surprised me (although, of course, I should have known better) was that, for every hundred people who express an interest, maybe only 6 out of that 100 will actually do something.

John Watts, a gentle family man, who volunteered to handle our finances, made the most important statement of the evening - 'Doing nothing is no longer an option'. He continued, 'We just can't go on as we are doing today. We've got to do something to change it.' He seemed to be tapping into something very deep down, almost coming up from the earth itself.

We've had contacts from all over the world. We ask people to either become a Supporter (someone who will take an active part in what we are seeking to do, and will receive our regular newsletter), or to be a Connector (someone who tries to arrange meetings and to start up a local group to further the project).

We knew we had a very broad and ill-defined agenda, and we also realised that if we were going to have any real impact we would need to focus on certain issues that were central to the philosophy of the PC.

The first fairly explosive issue we chose to take up was the debate about the Codex Alimentarius (CA). The public didn't know what the CA was, but the architects of this scheme started work on it 53 years earlier, and it concerned food and health supplements. The big pharmaceutical companies got together with the big agrichemical companies, and they seemed to be aiming to control everything we eat and everything we ingest - in pill form or in food form. To me, it seemed quite sinister.

The World Health Organisation (WHO) ostensibly set up the Codex Alimentarius to 'harmonise the feeding of the world' - 'harm' being the operative word. (laughter) The WHO is not a government organisation, although most people assume it is.

Many of the items on the CA are natural products that we have had the right to use for thousands of years. The big corporations seem intent on crushing smaller suppliers of these products, in order to take over the whole supplements business.

I'm not saying that pharmaceutical companies don't do great work, but I feel the agenda of the people who run these huge companies are highly suspect. I am clearly not alone.

In his 2008 Press Release, Hamish explained the rationale of The PC :-

'There's an exciting, positive force now acting around the world, releasing many millions of people from the illusion that the present system of rule by corporate bodies through their political partners - and the judicious use of funding to produce desired results - is so strong and well established that as individuals we can do nothing about it.

It is a matter of record that past structures with military, political or religious structures are notoriously short lived in real terms. In order to sustain and increase its influence, each one in turn is under pressure to repress and destroy any opposition to its agenda. The inevitable result is corruption within the system.

In spite of a media which seeks to control through fear, by constantly bombarding us with news of a depressing world, with a violent, envious, greedy and unhappy population, the fact is that there are hundreds of thousands of groups of people around the world now actively working to refute this corporate image. Amongst those thousands is the Parallel Community.

Organisers of the Parallel Community

The Parallel Community is not trying to reinvent the wheel. It has been set up as a website and an association where individuals and groups from a number of countries have a platform to contact each other, share ideas and develop practical ways to stop the corporate paralysis, which is profoundly affecting our quality of life.'

As front-line subversives go, Miller was something of an enigma. He was warm, generous, quietly spoken and self-effacing in a way you couldn't imagine a Guevara or an Ashoka behaving. However, beneath the 'everyone's-favourite-uncle' image there lurked a robust strand of fearless determination. Part remodelled baggage, part invigorated enlightenment, part righteous anger. Somebody had to do something - and it fell to Hamish to be that somebody.

The direction of action

There is a widespread belief that a global, corporate world, both public and private, has emerged that is out of touch with the private individual - and out of our control. The PC is set up to link together all the people at the bottom end, who are isolated - not only from the powers above, but from each other. Hamish came to understand that while we have a global economy, we still have individual sovereign governments. Many of the elected elements of the current system are actually puny in relation to the size and power of the unelected corporate organisations. The United Nations has been in place for many decades, in effect to try to link the governments up and to promote beneficial aims and objectives worldwide. People further down have never had that opportunity. The Parallel Community has the objective of joining those people to one another.

> I think we've got to change our own ground rules. If you read the popular press, you will get the impression at the moment that 90% of humans are right bastards - and that's just not true. It's purely and simply that we have a media, a financial system and some big companies that are obsessed with making money - seemingly for it's own sake. It doesn't leave room for any of the valuable, but intangible, things that are not quantifiable by accountants. The ability to do things, priceless spiritual things, has no value to bean counters or business people - nor does the quality of life of their workforce.

As someone who started my working life as an accountant (and I am still technically a qualified accountant) it is sometimes uncomfortable to hear this said. Yet I have been too close to too many for whom this commonplace caricature is all too valid.

Hamish, the former high-flying businessman, had a unique perspective on the role and the impact of commerce and industry. He knew that not everyone in the material world was selfish and self-obsessed - but those who longed for something more hopeful forever seemed to be working against the grain.

> I know there are some businessmen who are trying to make a positive difference, but they are stuck in a global financial structure that works against the better qualities of human endeavour. I'm mainly talking about the big conglomerates, run by people who have no perception of fairness or compassion about people at all.
>
> The trouble is that they have a huge influence over the way the species is heading. We have been led to believe that we're all wicked and we're all greedy - and the present system plays on that illusion. To keep the current framework in place, it needs us to think that way - but I don't agree with the religious fundamentalists; I don't believe we're intrinsically terrible. There's a huge percentage of the world's population who are really good spiritual beings, who only want to live happily with their family, bring up their kids,

be warm and clothed - and maybe move on to doing something more enlightening. These absolute basics have been completely forgotten, because of the actions and marketing approaches of the conglomerates. There is a much deeper value to the human spirit than the making of yet more cluster bombs. It's that sort of morality that is destroying the perception of the direction that the human species could take.

However, I think there's a massive strength in the huge number of people who want a different future. It's a number that's growing all the time - and that's why I think it's <u>so</u> important to get the message over about the subtle energies of association between humans and between human groups. Together, they are infinitely more powerful than the amoral multinationals. In essence, all we have to do is to get together and say, very simply, to them. 'Sorry, we're not going to buy your product.'

These people thrive when they sell us something. If enough people stand up, as they did with GM crops, and say 'No, we're not having that!', then we can avoid the dreadful future that many of the larger organisations would wish upon us.

With the growth of insidious technological processes, such as nanotechnology, we could be moving towards a situation where the whole species is under the control of a few powerful people. Even though I wouldn't subscribe to a conspiracy theory as such, it does worry me.

On the other hand, there are so many people who are becoming aware of the issues that it's setting in motion a groundswell of concern. There is a growing awareness of the subtle influences of these companies, which makes me believe that we'll be able to do something about it this time, but maybe only by a whisker!

The response to somebody who tells you you've got to go to war with Iran - or anywhere else for that matter - is clear. We've got to say to them 'That's <u>your</u> product, <u>you</u> go. We're not going.' We have to develop the courage to do just that.

> I repeat, the simplest way for the person in the street to contribute to the harnessing of the conglomerates is to say 'We're not going to buy your product'.

There are 'parallel' organisations in other countries, but few of them have the approach of the Parallel Community. Most of them have latched on to one particular angle or support one or other specific cause. For example, The AVAARZ in the US is able to drum up significant funding, which tends to be used for anti-governmental campaigns. In one sense, it's an equivalent entity. It's based on a web approach, where members can vote and support petitions and it's a source of finance for those fighting the dominance of Big Finance and Big Politics. There is a further similarity, in that they appear to be just a small number of people, who are working their socks off, representing a wider movement to try to make the world a better place. The PC has links with them, and generally supports their agenda. However, as yet, there is nothing quite like the Parallel Community.

Opening hearts and minds

The experience of the last few decades is that however genuine your intentions and however strong your motivation, change comes slowly. When progress is made, it comes in manageable little chunks. Many, many people, even the young and enthusiastic, deep down hate and fear change. To avoid frightening your own horses, it seems that the only way to make any positive progress at all is to support small incremental steps. It could be described as an evolutionary, rather than a revolutionary, approach.

The faltering improvement in racial and sexual equality are two classic cases of enlightenment by numbers - one court case, one petition, one referendum at a time. Links form between groups with common ground, and those who supported one cause can often be persuaded to support another. The whole social model jerks slowly and intermittently forward. However, without an overall philosophy, each battle becomes a war of its own and each new campaign has to start from scratch.

The local Member of Parliament for Hamish's constituency summed up the received wisdom quite succinctly by describing the approach of the Parallel Community as having 'far too broad a canvas'. His advice, whilst generally supportive of the ethos of the fledgling organisation, was for it to concentrate on a few initiatives at a time. The members of the Parallel Community have a wider, and wilder, ambition.

It is often said that in order to make any lasting progress we need to win over the 'hearts and minds' of an intangible threshold of people at a philosophical level. Most people will react to immediate stimuli - financial crises, energy shortages, wildlife devastation - yet, when the next choice has to be made, many revert to type. It is something of an uphill task, to put it mildly, persuading people who have become accustomed to acquiring goods and services almost exclusively on price, that there are other dimensions to consider, that are cunningly obscured by the consumer marketing.

The same person who is understandably concerned about the fate of dolphins, to the extent that they will help to finance the safeguarding of these magnificent creatures, will often think little of buying tuna from the cheapest source. In so doing they may well be nullifying any benefit from their charitable donation. Of course, life is rarely as simple or as clear-cut as that, and finding enough sound information on complex issues, when it is wickedly manipulated by the advertising arms of trans-global corporations, is certainly one of the prime difficulties. However, even when faced with a definable choice, we are so unused to taking into account where a product has been made, from what, by whom, and under what circumstances, that most of us don't even think to ask.

The Fair Trade and Organic movements have made some progress in recent years, at least amongst the more open minded, but they still represent just a speck on the edge of the organisation of world trade. The PC seeks to unite some of these disparate elements into a credible, alternative, parallel set of communities.

In terms of reaching hearts and minds, I was given a unique opportunity to study this process at close quarters - indeed it was thrust at me in a way that, in hindsight, looks like an obligatory part of my personal development. By a series of co-incidences and mishaps, I ended up helping to implement one of the first major Green Staff Travel Plans in the UK, at Derriford Hospital in Plymouth. The details of the plan itself and the remarkable achievements, set against a background of vitriolic hostility, could easily be the subject of a book in itself.

For this purpose, it is sufficient to note that the hospital achieved in the order of a 15% - 20% shift by its staff from less sustainable transport modes to more sustainable modes. This remains one of the most substantial shifts of transport behaviour anywhere in the UK. With the press and the workforce staunchly against anything that threatened the 'right to drive to work', the team managed to win over enough people to at least give something else a chance. Despite being a former car factory worker myself, I had had no personal experience of the strength and depth of the motor and oil industry lobby until we started to suggest, rather radically as it turned out, that some people might like to catch a bus occasionally. The hospital was centralising at an alarming speed and a change of government policy, which (for once) at least recognised the onrushing problem of traffic congestion, resulted in a planning refusal for a hugely enlarged car park. This, in turn, left a considerable shortfall of the anticipated permitted parking, based on historical trends. With only a few months to go to the opening of important new regional facilities, it was apparent that if the number of cars coming to the site rose in line with conventional expectations, traffic chaos would ensue - potentially threatening the very operation of the hospital itself. So, we hired the best Consultant we could afford and . . . prayed.

The basis of the Green Staff Travel Scheme, based on a similar scenario that had worked well in Seattle in the US, was that a modest car-parking fee (initially just 20p a day) was to be introduced - and all the revenue gained would be recycled to subsidise bus fares. There was some hope that at least the less well off members of staff would be more likely to catch a bus with the attraction of a cheaper season ticket. Even at the time, it didn't seem exactly red-hot revolutionary, and looking back it seems barely tepid, but hell hath no fury like the theoretically threatened driver. Despite being a lifelong football supporter, and quite used to the quaint vernacular of the terraces, in the first few days that the Travel Plan went live, I had never heard such a torrent of verbal abuse, spat out with such vehemence by my fellow professionals, in all my life.

However, after a few weeks, with the introduction of a balanced portfolio of measures, supported by a lot of consultation and a lot of patience, we got to a point where the hospital was still open and the parking levy grudgingly accepted. The buses were filling up and the route network expanding.

In an unexpected turn of events, much later on, I was encouraged to embark on a strange study tour of UK public sector sites, explaining what we had achieved and why most of us were still alive to tell the tale. Only then did I get the chance to analyse what had been happening during the traumatic weeks leading up to the start of the Green Travel Plan. Only then did I realise that we had stumbled on some of the most profound issues, not only of transport planning, but of what makes people tick and what makes them act.

Some commuters certainly changed modes for financial reasons alone, or because they were actively prevented from taking their first choice of transport mode. But the factor that actually made the whole scenario work, against a background of such antagonism, was that we had, almost inadvertently, won over the hearts and minds of a significant minority of those affected. These were people who understood what we were trying to achieve; why we were taking this allegedly draconian course of action - and they were with us. Often silently, often reluctantly, they were starting to see the world in a different way - and so was I. It was, as Hamish would have said, a cathartic moment.

I came to the conclusion that, in any given cross section of the population, about 15% - 20% of the people were positively with you anyway - and just needed help, support and information. At the other end of the spectrum, 15% - 20% were so dead set against you that any time you spent talking to them was time wasted. They could only see the world through the narrow focus of the individual in the here and now - it seemed sad, but so be it. Between these two groups was 60% - 70% of those affected, who were, to a greater or lesser extent, persuadable, providing you were open, transparent and honest. It was this group that saved the hospital from the downward spiral of chaos and recrimination - and it is this group that potentially <u>can</u> save the wider society from itself.

Whether Hamish's colleagues can mobilise the goodwill that we essentially, yet completely unexpectedly, chanced upon in the caring heart of the community, time alone will tell.

Hamish did have the advantage of being eternally optimistic, whereas those of us at the hospital thought we were all going to be sacked when the ridiculously audacious scheme failed - if we weren't to be burnt alive by our colleagues first. Indeed, the first day that the Travel Plan went live, I had a string of phone calls from across the UK. Ostensibly, these calls were from people who were casually asking about how things were going - but I had a suspicion that they were really calling to find out if we still existed.

Challenging the cult of insular individualism

Just about every movement that has come into existence with the avowed intent of stemming the tide of corporate suffocation, has made the assumption that the recreation of local societies, based on local accountability and responsibility, is the way forward. It is taken for granted that people actually want to work in groups with those who surround them. The emerging buzzword 'localism' seeks to wrap this concept up into a soundbite. There is a further assumption that these people have similar goals and similar (largely unspoken) social objectives.

Our intuition tells us that this is an obviously desirable direction of travel. Yet, as anyone who has ever tried to run a local fete, let alone a mass social movement, will tell you, the translation of rhetoric into action can be a brittle transition. It is interesting to hear, therefore, that with a little help, the Parallel Community seems to be surmounting this barrier. People are emerging, almost on cue, in a way that gives legs to Hamish's sense of being guided.

There is a great British tradition of baking cakes and rattling tins, even of writing articles and books, in support of positive goals. Long may that continue. But the alchemy of making the conversion from righteous indignation to a groundswell of commitment can be as elusive as . . . an explanation of dowsing to the sceptic.

Although many of us rail against the direction of the society we are building, we've got what we've got because somebody, indeed lots of somebodies, actually wanted it. People latched on to the comfort and the convenience of isolation and materialism - and they found that it suited them.

As I mentioned at the start of this story, I almost literally grew up in a sweet shop. My family saw the advent of impersonal self-service supermarkets wipe out lots of our corner shops in the 1960's and 1970's. My parents' 'mom 'n' pop' store survived largely because it was too far away from the cavernous cashier to be too badly affected - but with improving road transport and the ever greater purchasing power of the retail oligarchy, their successors were less fortunate.

Undoubtedly, the lower prices and wider product choice of the supermarkets were some of the understandable reasons for the transition. However, there was also a hidden attraction at the new retail outlets. People could select and purchase their necessary provisions for themselves - without ever having to engage with anyone. They appreciated the fact that they could do their shopping without ever having to talk to or to deal with another living soul. It is another unwelcome elephant in the room for those of us who see the redemption of local communities as essential to revitalising the human condition, that so many people welcome the freedom to live their lives in almost total isolation - at least to the extent that they can avoid any meaningful interaction.

I came up against this same issue when trying to promote sustainable transport. While the public debate about the pros and cons of buses and trains is a niche world in itself - and well beyond the scope of a book like this - one of the core issues that made a positive modal shift towards sustainability so difficult to achieve was the deep-seated desire to avoid unnecessary contact. The loneliness of the long-distance car journey, buoyed up by personal privacy, the comfort of the air-con and the company of the MP3, is the devil we know and love.

On the surface, the arrival of Facebook, My Space and other social networking sites should have heralded a new era of multiple friendships. Most young people, with 30-50 fellow-travellers on their databases, seem to be far better connected and far more involved than sad souls like myself, who probably never had more than half a dozen mates at any given time. Yet, social networking is so satisfying precisely because it can be carried out at a safe distance. If you decide you no longer like someone or you feel they're trying to come a bit too close, you can just delete them. I am sure there have been times when we would all have loved to have done just that. However, if you know you are going to meet those people at local events, in the pub or at the corner shop, personal relationships become much more complex.

Even Hamish, the standard bearer of the New Way of Life, had to admit that when faced with a room full of tables, some of which were occupied, and others not, he would usually choose a vacant one. It's no shame; I'm with him all the way, but it does sound a warning bell about unmarked shipwrecks below the waves of society.

In the culture we have cultured, the ethic of individualism has very strong roots. So many of us are used and conditioned to seeing ourselves as separate from everything and everybody else.

For those, like Ba, who have the self-confidence and the open heartedness to see themselves primarily as part of a society, the world must look so different. They are part of the committed 20% who have the embodied vision of a positive society that can help to create the scaffolding of a workable Parallel Community. The rest of us will need a little more encouragement.

It is important here not to be confused between individuality - the ability to contribute in our own personal way to the world we inhabit - and individualism, which indicates that we only ever see that world from the inside looking out. There are many who have a decent panorama of their personal cosmos, but like the Victorian atlas, which was so distorted by placing the pink blob of Britain slap in the middle of a receding horizon, they place themselves at the heart of the sun. It's not self-aggrandisement; it just seems like common sense; the way things are. On one level, we may have accepted that the earth does go round the sun - but so many people still seem pretty sure that the known universe circles around themselves.

Excessive individualism expresses itself in many ways, some more subtle than others. We are all aware of the egocentricity of youth that fails to understand that the world around them is not an inanimate plaything; this expresses itself in alienation, vandalism and antisocial behaviour. I doubt if anyone reading this book can put hand on heart and say they have never been there at some point.

In later years, those who have yet to work it through fully, display similar traits as aggression, selfishness and profiteering. However, despite the most strenuous efforts of corporate capitalism to keep us ensnared in a whirlpool of consumption, competitiveness and debt, most of us surface from time to time to realise that all this is madness. On some level, we do appreciate that there is more to life than buying gadgets and watching soaps - some even escape the downward drag altogether and occasionally become a useful member of society. However, all too many lose sight of the wider world and become mired in a revolving door of fear, insecurity and a siege mentality.

But it is not just the physical and social levels of existence that are degraded by excessive self-protection. At an energetic level, too much emphasis on the needs of the self cuts us off from the help we can give and obtain from others. We can so easily become tiny, self-obsessed pieces of driftwood tumbling through the turbulent vortices of the ocean of intangible forces.

Hamish's dowsing work showed that we are all deeply, irrevocably interconnected by the subtle - and the not so subtle - forces that can be demonstrated and measured. There is nothing airy-fairy about this; it's just nature in the raw. Everything we do, and probably everything we think, has an effect, however tiny, on everything and everybody else. Similarly, everybody else's actions and energies affect us. It is the hackneyed (but illustrative) idea of the flapping of a butterfly's wings in the rainforest that, through a chain of unlikely but not impossible actions, brings down a government in Europe.

Hamish's dowsing of auras also supported this view at a slightly different level. The seven auras that surround the body, which can easily be dowsed by a comparative novice, indicate that the physical body is just one of our relationships with the wider world. The other auras fan out, depending on our health and spiritual development, way beyond our visible form. We are all therefore interconnected, to the extent that we share the same space with a myriad of other entities - at exactly the same time. We overlap, intertwine, intermingle. We are inescapably part of a tangled tapestry of subtle energies. Maybe this is precisely why we strive so hard to work out who or what we really are - and fight so hard to protect it - whatever 'it' actually is.

The individualism we see promoted around us may well be just the social expression of this much deeper-seated malaise. Imbalances at an energetic level may be leaving us fearful of change, fearful of a future we can't comprehend. Hamish's work with The Management sought to unpick and rectify some of these imbalances. More importantly, his insights enable anyone to see themselves as an active and constructive part of an infinitely complex cosmos of which myself, yourself, The Management and their Management are all a part.

The Parallel Community may have its work cut out to cope with such profound and entrenched individualism, but at least with Hamish's initial momentum, they will have a fighting chance.

A recurring theme

Only when we were piecing together the various elements of Hamish's life and work, did he come to appreciate that the urge to form an organisation that could further the aims of the positive-thinking members of the global society was embedded in his own previous experience. As we saw earlier, in the early 1980's, shortly after his NDE, Hamish joined Colin Bloy's Brighton-based Fountain Group. This was, and still is, a worldwide community of like-minded individuals who strive to make the world a better place by the collective healing of the lands they inhabit. Hamish was clearly proud to be part of this initiative - and Ba still attends its functions in his stead.

In 1986, the Alphega Manifesto of the Fountain Group (see extracts at Appendix C) was declared by HM in Andorra - a tiny landlocked country, high in the Pyrenees, surrounded by France and Spain. And why, of all places, Andorra?

The Cathars were a heretical religious sect based in Southern France, which was violently suppressed by the King of France, at the behest of the Pope. Their last stand, and the massacre of every Cathar man, woman and child by their Christian persecutors was at Montsegur, which is now a place of pilgrimage for those of a spiritual inclination. There is a legend that the night before the final slaughter, something of their ancient secret knowledge was somehow smuggled out of the besieged fortress by four of their members.

Colin came to understand that - somewhere - there was a very special stone that could cause pictograms to appear in the earth's energy field. He couldn't define exactly what they were because he didn't know what they were himself at that time. In an effort to locate this important stone, Colin consulted the great, unsung dowser Bill Lewis. I think that Bill was one of the best map dowsers there has ever been. He admitted, quite wryly, that he became an expert map dowser primarily because his wife didn't like him staying away from home. So he did most of his dowsing in the kitchen, where he got a huge amount of practice.

Colin gave Bill the vaguest of briefs that somewhere in Europe (think about it!) there was a particular stone, which he felt had some relationship with the Cathar movement in southern France. More than that he did not know. Colin felt he was getting the message that it was up to him to find it.

Not surprisingly, it was some months before Bill came back to him. Eventually, however, he rang Colin to tell him that he felt the stone was in Andorra - and gave him the name of a village. In the corner of that village there was a restaurant with a balcony - so, he was actually remote viewing. Bill told him that he would need to climb up the hill behind the restaurant, and that there he would find a little cave. He would need to dig in that cave and there he would find the stone.

The story is that Colin went to the village, found the restaurant, climbed up the hill and found the cave. He dug into the floor of the cave for two or three hours with a trowel, but he was bitterly disappointed because he couldn't find anything of significance at all. Then it occurred to him that he might be looking for a much bigger stone than might have been the case. So, he sifted through all the rubble he had dug out - and finally found a stone that was quite small. He dowsed it with his hands and he realised that that was indeed the one he had been looking for.

After he started working with it, he sensed that it wanted to be transported back to Montsegur. Consequently, he took it to the former Cathar fortress, where he used it to dowse a message at the foot of the cliffs, where all the remaining Cathars had been killed.

Later he took the stone back to Andorra, where he used it to discover many of the energy pictograms around the village church. He brought it back to the UK, where he used it to dowse similar pictograms around Shipley church, near to Ba's house in Sussex. That church had been a Templar preceptory - and the Templars were closely associated with the Cathars, who seemed to know a lot about the impacts and benefits of earth energy.

Colin spent several days in and around Shipley church with the stone, which triggered these pictograms. He spent some time drawing up a map showing all the pictograms that he could find. While he was there, he explained what he was doing to a monk, who also happened to be visiting the church. The monk told him that he didn't need to explain what he was finding as he, the monk, could see the pictograms quite clearly! So, Colin asked him if he had got his map drawn up correctly. The monk was able to enhance the plan for him by adding sections he had missed, which Colin was then able to confirm by dowsing with the stone. The energy of the stone seemed to be interacting with both the energy of the place and the consciousness of the dowser to produce the pictograms.

It was an extraordinary story. Indeed, at the time I wasn't certain that it was completely kosher, as it seemed just too extraordinary. As you know, it's very important to retain a healthy scepticism about such things.

Before he left England for Spain, Colin left me with a rough photocopy of the manifestations he dowsed around the stone.

Pictograms drawn by Colin Bloy

Wherever he was, he could use the stone to trigger these manifestations in the ether.

It might have been a tool he was able to use to get his own mind into an appropriate state of consciousness to experience these phenomena.

In the end, he came to realize that the stone was not his to keep, nor even to use, and he felt very strongly that it should go back to where he had found it, so that other people could use it in the future. So, he took it back to Andorra. In fact, he found himself so attracted to the country that he bought a flat there.

It may well be that the 'treasure of the Cathars' was in fact this modest stone that was smuggled out the night before their holocaust. It had to be something small to have been removed silently in the darkness. It was a stone of remarkable qualities that could enable the bearer to observe the pictograms wherever they were. It was almost like a modern laptop computer, except of course that it was an artefact produced by the earth, rather than by man. You could regard it as a touchstone; a virtual key that unlocked the portal between the physical world and the dimension of earth energy.

It wasn't treasure as we would usually think of it - jewellery, gold or precious items - it was a treasury of knowledge, of insight. The idea that it was an item of great physical value is actually a very good cover story - almost designed to put those of bad intent off the trail of the real McCoy.

Hamish reading out the Alphega Manifesto

Colin asked me to read out his Alphega Manifesto in Andorra, close to the cave where the stone was found. It marked the start of a new phase of the development of the Fountain Group, moving on from just sensing earth energy and giving healing to the earth. I willingly agreed to be the announcer. When we arrived there, there were about 60 people from all over France, Spain and the UK. Colin had dowsed a suitable place for the proclamation. It was on a headland - a very powerful energy centre - and I bellowed out this manifesto to the assembled multitude into a howling gale!

When you look at it now, the text seems almost Old Testament in flavour. Perhaps one of the reasons that Alphega didn't take off as it might have done was that it was too close to the Old Religion. In one sense, it was the bathwater we had already thrown out. People didn't want that sort of thing any more; they wanted a new way of acknowledging the underlying forces.

However, Colin himself never wanted to start a new religion - he never wanted be a guru. He was a frontiersman with wonderful ideas, but he didn't want to be the front man.

I was astonished, because he was such a good speaker and raconteur. His timing was exquisite; he should have been a comedian! He could tell the most mundane stories and everyone would be convulsed in laughter. I really envied that talent.

Barely 20 years on, the text of the manifesto seems oddly stilted, and not a little pompous. This is a salutary reminder of how quickly an evolution of mood overtakes the stance of even the most far-sighted of initiatives.

It is yet another example of someone having a vision of what could be achieved, if the societal consciousness could be prized open a little further - but in attempting to describe that revelation in the words of the workaday world, it collapses into the litany of the lumber-room. However, within that over-formalised declaration lay the seed of what was to become the Parallel Community.

As the Fountain movement grew, it became a genuinely international groundswell of hope. Stemming from the same surge of energy and motivation that brought Fountain into existence, the Parallel Community has effectively become a new green branch of this mature, but still thriving, tree of life.

The way ahead for the Parallel Community

The PC has a vast canvas and awesome aspirations. However, it does still have to operate in the 'real world', albeit in a parallel version of the Big Media construct. So, as it matures, the PC will need to develop concerted themes and strands to concentrate the energy of the group and to prevent it being dissipated into eddies and cul-de-sacs.

Hamish suggested: 'threads' or nodes of interest and focus - different areas of approaching the world problems we face. These need to be specified in our statement of aims. It can then be suggested that those who wish to may form a group to pursue a thread. On request, a section of the website can be opened up for each thread, with discussion boards and online resources. I suggest each group has a focaliser (love it - NT), who sets it in motion, edits and maintains that website-section. A group starts when there is someone to get it going!

Suggested threads might be:

world:	'world work', planetary healing, aid and holistic development
learning:	education, teaching (mainstream and alternative) and public awareness
green	ecology, climate, gardening, land-use, conservation, sustainability
people:	social work, activism, groups, people, education, public awareness
health:	healing, therapies, nutrition, conscious dying
politics:	political-social activism and issues, outreach, spreading the word
creativity:	arts, crafts, music, words, publishing, websites
spirit:	spiritual work and paths, mysteries, faiths, inner growth.

I think this approach might help get energy rising in PC, attracting a spectrum of different kinds of people.

Like a youngster furiously spinning a hoop, Hamish was determined to give the Parallel Community as much impetus as possible, right up to his very last minute. Those who have picked up the baton are only too aware of the need to maintain the momentum.

The PC appreciate that it's about engendering the actions required to promote an evolving world - instigating website threads, giving talks, writing articles, saving woodlands, saying 'No' to products and services we are unhappy about - and yet not forgetting to assist our elderly neighbour, not missing the beauty in every situation . . .

It's about the sense of the encompassing circular action, rather than the angular and linear path of the old way. It's about everyone making the tiny changes necessary for a very different tomorrow. It's about each member of Parallel Community connecting with another person, even if they are not yet part of PC, and progressively carrying out, and being seen to carry out, those actions that enable this growth to take place. It's about winning hearts and minds at a very elemental, yet everyday, level.

Hamish has prepared the ground; PC just needs to 'simplicate', as HM loved to say. It's not more speed or power that is required, but the realisation of the huge importance of his insight and intention and, using powerful direction, to hold the course that he has set - and to put it into practice. This is the team's work. It is growing daily, and growing internationally, in support of Hamish's vision.

Both the PC and myself know very much what he intended, yet we are all struggling to put it into words - which brings us back to the dilemma of the NDE survivor desperately trying to explain his amazing vision. The PC is about thinking and doing things in a totally different way. The yogi Krishnamurti's words seem very apt in this context. "You can't see what to do, you can see only what not to do. The total negation of that road is the new beginning, the other road. This other road is not on the map, nor can it ever be put on any map. Every map is a map of the wrong road, the old road." The new way is so much more liberating - because there is no road, just Hamish's new way of 'being the world'.

By the spring of 2010, the Parallel Community had over 1,000 supporters, and over 130 connectors, mainly based in the UK, but with a growing presence in Ireland, Holland, France, Germany, Spain, New Zealand, Canada and Guatemala.

Contact details are shown at Appendix B.

An Enlightened Future

What the future means, let alone what it holds, is a difficult concept to grasp in a dimension where time is of no consequence.

While those he has left behind may harbour a certain amount of concern for the way ahead, bordering on trepidation, for Hamish the next cycle was already anticipated with much hope, and not a little excitement.

Son of Sun and Daughter of Serpent

The Sun and the Serpent project had started out as a Dan Dare type adventure to test the theories of John Michell. It ended up unlocking a whole new way of understanding both the energy fields of which we are all a part, and also the spatial distribution of the ancient sites of human habitation.

What Hamish had never realised, and certainly never intended when he started his research, was that his work would spur others into action. People from various backgrounds and disciplines have not only followed in his footsteps, but also reinterpreted his findings in their own unique ways.

I am probably one of several thousand people across the world who, on reading *The Sun and the Serpent*, went out into the countryside to see what it was all about for myself.

Some years later, after the publication of *The Dance of the Dragon*, I wrote to Hamish, somewhat speculatively, to enquire if this mythical author had any intention of publishing his findings in map form - as he had already made available for *The Sun and the Serpent.* We were off to Greece later that year and it seemed a whizzo idea to try to find one of these lines somewhere abroad. I had expected to get some stuffy letter back from someone I assumed to be a reclusive academic, saying that they would be available from all good bookshops, at some point, at some extortionate fee. Instead, I got a polite, hand signed little note asking when we were going, so he could get the maps completed in time - which he duly did. I later published my own findings on the website of the Tamar Dowsers. I am sure we were not the only English eccentrics to have found Apollo and Athena in Athens and Delphi as a result of reading his books.

Yet, my involvement was little more than a repetition of his work -
actually just a personal verification that I wasn't being strung a line.
Others have taken it to a different level altogether.

By the end of the 1990's, word of the discovery of the earth energy
arteries was spreading across Europe. A German film crew from Munich
came over to the UK to investigate the mystery. In fact, they were
intending to make a video of the 1999 solar eclipse, as seen from
Trencrom Hill, and to show the route of the Michael/Mary 'ley' line. In
the end, the eclipse, as some of you may remember, was all but washed
out in Penwith, and the resulting video, Erdenlicht, was a bit of
something and nothing. However, it was significant that, even before *The
Dance of the Dragon* or *In Search of the Southern Serpent* had appeared
in print, a professional film crew was prepared to ship over lorry loads of
equipment, clearly at considerable cost, to visit the living legends of
Britain - Stonehenge, Avebury, Glastonbury - and Hamish Miller, on the
strength of reading *The Sun and the Serpent*.

Other videos featuring Hamish and his revelations have been made by
production companies from Holland, Sweden and Japan.

As time has gone by, others have also turned their intention to Michael
and Mary, often with unexpected results. A book with the working title
of *Balancing the Male and Female Energies* has been produced, featuring
the internationally renowned dancer, Frances Lewis, and the
photographer, Adelina Abad-Pedrosa. They were inspired by the ideas
brought to life by *The Sun and the Serpent* and Hamish has contributed a
Foreword to their work.

Frances Lewis

The interesting thing about
this whole book is that, in
dance, Frances has
interpreted the subtleties of
the Michael and Mary earth
energy lines. She has danced
at each of the major crossing
points along the route. To me,
this is a huge breakthrough -
and it's very, very moving. It's
so humbling, because I didn't
realise that people were latching on to the essence of

what we discovered in this way. The book is a lavish production, and although it may never be printed in any great quantity, it's a quite magnificent work.

In a similar vein, but with a rather different outlook, came the project called the *Awakening Albion* walk.

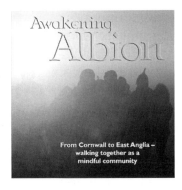

'In early May 2008, a group of pilgrims watched the Beltane sunrise from a cliff top headland near Lands End, and then set out on a journey ... on foot ... across southern England. Following the path of the Michael/Mary ley line, they walked the sacred and mythological landscape that is Albion. Nearly fifty days (and over 500 miles) later, they reached the Norfolk coast in time to witness the Summer Solstice sunrise over the North Sea. A celebration of the land's beauty, as well as a witnessing of its wounding, the Walk was also a powerful experience of community for all involved. This book tells the story of that journey in photographs, drawings, poems and diary entries.'

Given that the journeys that Hamish made with his various collaborators became spiritual undertakings in their own right, the comparison with the essence of Chaucer's *Pilgrims Progress* seems unavoidable.

I have a sense of wonder and humility that so many people have, after 20 years, reacted to the book and to the subtle energies of the earth. It's just incredibly rewarding. It's an indication that what we're doing isn't an airy-fairy enterprise; it's having a profound effect. I feel it's all part of enabling people to experience a different range of perceptions of what's possible. If I have opened a few doors somewhere along the way, that's very gratifying.

. . . and yet more progeny:

Julian Marshall, the well known pop and classical composer, was so intrigued by *The Sun and the Serpent* that he wrote and performed a piece of music about it. It's only about seven minutes long, but it's quite beautiful.

Julian Marshall

He actually ran a series of Master Classes using the Michael and Mary energy. He had about eight people on each of them and they included choreographers, composers, dancers or instrumentalists. During the weekend, he would take them to the Hurlers stone circles, where the energies cross and interact. I used to meet them there. I would ask them to choose a stone - and to interpret the energy of that stone as they felt it - in music, dance or whatever their chosen discipline was.

He then took the process one stage further. He would hold the class at another location, and during one of the sessions he would show them a picture of Twelve o' Clock Rock, which is quite close to my home. They had to concentrate for a while in their own way on the photograph of the rock and then to interpret that energy as they thought fit. I asked him to set this up at any time, providing it was on the hour, any hour after 12.00, on the Sunday of the Master Class. I would go up to the rock each hour and dowse to find out if there was any reaction to be felt there. The results were absolutely extraordinary; four out of the five times we tried it, the radials coming out of that stone at least doubled at the time of the event, and not at any other hour. I didn't know which of the available times they would choose and I didn't even know if anything would happen at all. It was a double-blind experiment. Yet a group of people, concentrating on a photograph of Twelve o' Clock Rock, which they had probably never even seen in situ, were measurably affecting the energetic activity of that stone from many, many miles away. The beauty of knowing the energy signature of a location well is that you can tell when it's being affected by something out of the ordinary.

Some time later, Julian suggested that I went to teach 'his children' to dowse. I thought he meant his own children, but when I arrived he had assembled a couple of the classes from the local village school. There were about 60 pupils.

It was quite a cathartic experience for me, because some of the children were only about seven. So, I tried to pitch my talk about vibrations and frequencies in terms that I thought might mean something to these youngsters. I was just staggering into an explanation about how natural and man-made frequencies can affect their minds, when a little lad in the front row, wearing an oversized peaked golfing hat, put his hand up and asked 'Excuse me, are you talking about alpha rhythms?' So I immediately upped the level of the talk!

Some of them picked it up so well, they were dowsing at lunchtime as to whether they should be eating the food - or not!

All this stemmed from the inspiration generated by the Sun and the Serpent project.

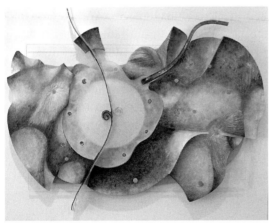

Langstone Down - Mary line running through centre cairn - by Peter Bousfield

Yet another emanation inspired by the energy lines rediscovered by Hamish is the work of artist and member of the Tamar Dowsers, Peter Bousfield. Peter has used his understanding of the impact of the Mary Line energy on the topography of the landscape near where he lives, on the edge of Bodmin Moor in East Cornwall, to produce a series of multi-media artworks. The result is a unique and striking interpretation of how energy and matter interact.

On another occasion, an ex-naval man who, as a means of getting his life back together after his marriage broke up, walked the Michael/Mary lines with his dog. He produced a book, which I found hilariously funny, which was partly in his dialogue and partly with the dog talking. However, as there was no textual differentiation between the two narrators, you have to work it out for yourself. Most of it is self-evident of course, but there are places where it could be either of them talking. At one point he was describing some of the people he met in Glastonbury, and the text reads to the effect that 'if this lady doesn't stop fondling about, I'll bite her fingers off'.

His way of getting his life back together was to do something insane - like taking his dog for a walk for the full length of the Michael/Mary caduceus.

In a similar vein, one day, a Danish chap turned up at Treviscoe to tell Hamish that he had just started walking the lines. Hamish was concerned about this man because he noticed that the Dane's boots were virtually hanging off his feet. He advised his visitor that he couldn't walk any distance in boots like that. There seemed to be a real danger that he'd never make it. So, as a stopgap, Hamish found an old pair of his own sandals that were pretty far-gone and gave them to him. The walker put them on and left his old boots behind. Weeks later, a lady called from somewhere near Reading to say that she'd been out walking in the countryside near her house and had met this same chap. In the conversation, it came up that he was still wearing HM's old shoes. As a result of this conversation, sometime later she went to visit Hamish and Ba and enjoyed a pleasant afternoon talking about their mutual experiences with the Michael and Mary lines.

There seem to be a huge number of similarly tenuous connections that have been sparked off by the revelations in *The Sun and the Serpent*.

Another shoot off the Michael/Mary rootstock is the work of the cellist Fredi Alberti, who used to place the spike of his cello in the middle of an energy centre. I have dowsed some of these places before and after his interpretation of the energy there and the impact of the music can be extraordinary. In some locations, the energy spiral has wound itself up like a clock spring, while at others it would wind itself out. The fascinating thing, of course, is that it responds to sound vibration at all.

The follow up from *The Sun and the Serpent* wasn't exclusively complimentary. When the author and dowser, Paul Deveraux, held the role of Ley Hunter-in-Chief, he wasn't at all enthusiastic about Hamish's initial work on the wiggly lines. As a Ley Hunter, Paul was very much a straight-line man. During his period, a strip cartoon started to appear in the journal *The Ley Hunter*. It featured a bloke with a big beard and huge dowsing rods, which was clearly intended to be Hamish - and it ran for several months. Perversely, Hamish was rather chuffed about this, because as far as he knows, he is the only dowser ever to have featured in a strip cartoon! You know you have made the big time when you are famous enough to be worth lampooning in the press - even if it's in a niche publication like *The Ley Hunter*. Despite the leg-pulling, Paul and Hamish became admirers of one another's work.

Cartoon by Sib Cole/Wyvern Dowsers 1995

One of the things I am only just coming to terms with is the fact that the discovery of the Michael and Mary lines was a more significant breakthrough than I had ever imagined. After 20 years, it seems to be still growing; indeed it seems to be coming of age. People have bought more maps covering the Michael and Mary lines this last year (2009) than in the last five put together.

This idea of discoveries coming of age, or coming to light at a time when they can be taken on board, deserves more consideration. It pays to stand back and look at these insights with the deeper perspective of hindsight afforded to other significant breakthroughs in the fields of science or philosophy. At the time that Einstein was publishing his heretical works or Newton was banging on about gravity, no one outside a little circle of cognoscenti thought much of them. The man or woman in the street would probably not even have heard about such ideas for many years - and when they did, they would have dismissed them as the work of idle dreamers. However, a few decades later their significance was recognised and they have now become important parts of the foundation of how we understand the world around us.

It may seem a little premature to put HM on the same plinth as these leviathans, but history has a funny way of choosing its heroes. Perhaps because time, or at least our perception of it, seems to be speeding up, so the lag between discovery and acceptance may be decreasing. The audience for any concept has to have the mental framework and the intellectual thirst to be able to absorb it. In the case of such a paradigm-threatening concept as earth energy, with such knock-on practical importance, perhaps it needed a longer gestation. Perhaps, too, at the time it first appeared in the written media the idea was just too revolutionary to be accepted at face value. However, a couple of decades later, it's starting to sink in with a new generation just what this 'ordinary bloke' unearthed. Despite having taken twenty-odd years to break through the surface, once out into the volatile atmosphere of everyday thinking . . .

There were a few people who read *The Sun and The Serpent* when it first appeared who realised that these guys were on to something of great significance, but most would probably have dismissed it as little more than a whimsical flight of fancy. Even the participants were blissfully unaware of the implications of what they were revealing.

> At the time, I was in total innocence about what was going on. I was astonished and intrigued - and there was a realisation that this must have a deeper meaning behind it - but I had no idea what - and I certainly had no idea of the ramifications.

Moving on up

In the run-up to his passing over, Hamish was all too aware that his next destination would be a very different way-station, even if it was not an entirely foreign land:

> Beyond the veil is a place to which I am looking forward to returning. It's somewhere with which I feel almost familiar. I have an extraordinary sensation that part of me stayed there on my first sojourn, waiting for the rest of me to come back!
>
> I'm familiar, if you like, with the way of getting there and I'm familiar with some of the concepts I'm likely to meet - and I'm 100% sure that when you do move off this mortal coil, your essence or soul or call it what you like, is a complete unit which retains all the memories of all the lifetimes you have ever had. You become reunited with your past. In that sense, you'll reclaim great tracts of your greater self.
>
> You might think you've done fairly well in this life, but when you get to where you're going and you realise what the class above can do with all their extra senses, you'll become aware that you're going to have to start all over again. It's great; I'm really looking forward to that.

In the future that Hamish had already glimpsed, there is no future - or any past for that matter. Life, for want of a better description, just 'is'. Time is a sort of illusion, invented by man to make sense of the physical world we are passing through. When HM was telling me this, I had a cameo vision of the Dalai Lama, nodding sagely, but with a concealed, endearing little smile.

The brush with The Management left Hamish with the firm view that we remain as individuated entities over a myriad of lifetimes, until we finally accumulate enough understanding, and unburden enough misunderstanding, to move on. His impression of the next level up was that it would require a quantum jump from where he had reached in this cycle - and that presumably he would be obliged to go round quite a few more times before the end of the escalator allowed him to step off into somewhere he could handle. However, he was by no means disconsolate at this fate, and he saw it as a necessary part of his development.

While the view forward seemed pretty clear to him, when it came to accessing past lives, Hamish reserved judgement. He tried a past life regression once, during which he was allegedly a team leader of a stone-moving cadre. While he was clearly impressed with the clarity of his vision, I could tell by the tone of his voice that he was not entirely convinced by the authenticity of the experience. Like me, he was deeply sceptical of the fact that an improbable proportion of the people who choose to undergo such regressions find they have been Pharaohs (of which there were only a few) or Marie Antoinette (of which there was only one). The implication is that people may indeed be accessing a valid historical record, but not necessarily their own. The availability, under certain conditions, of the Akashic Records - the trace in the ether in which the experience of all existence can be viewed, or even brought into consciousness - could also indicate a potential flaw in the standard regression process. That said, Hamish was quite clear that when he had the chance to stay 'upstairs' or to return to carry through this cycle, he had the availability of all of his previous life experiences against which to make that judgement.

His impression of the Big Picture was that there are a vast number of stages of potential personal progress, of which the floor above, where the current members of The Management are in temporary residence, is just one of many. His view was that people retain their individual identity until they reach a much deeper level of awareness, at which point they may 'merge with the divine' or however the philosophy of your choice tries to describe such an ineffable destination.

Hamish became a firm believer that the upward path is something you choose to take when you are ready. You can seek advice from a guide or a guru - physical or spiritual - but the decision to take the first step has to be yours alone. You have to feel the need to do it for yourself. You have to move your own feet.

Various philosophies put forward the view that the way forward is to take on board the distilled and collected wisdom of someone else, albeit someone more enlightened. Hamish was unequivocally dismissive of this. To him, that was just kidding yourself. Sometimes, others can certainly help you; they can point you in the right direction; they can certainly give you a kick start (as Michael and Colin did for him) - but only when you have come to embody what it means, are you able to evolve personally.

Just as the Buddhist sage leaves the bewildered pilgrim with no more than a riddle that says 'just think about it', so Colin Bloy's 'do-it-yourself' rebuff to Hamish's desire to short-cut the path to sensitivity was the only meaningful response.

Hamish had no time for those ways of thinking that rely on the benevolence of an intermediary. For the former entrepreneur, the creation of your own enlightened reality is down to self-help and hard work.

A dynamic future

Even for those with the benefit of an advanced snapshot, the vision of the future changes with the angle of the watcher. Everyone at any big sporting event sees the game in a subtly different way - some see it foreshortened, while others see the big picture, but without much detail. Your standpoint determines the perspective and your baggage chooses the lens through which you view it.

By the time I arrived on this plane as yours-truly, six years of the future had passed since the end of WWII. Britain had had the chance to feel euphoria mellow into relief; for the excitement of the brave new world to become a little more mundane. Disillusion was creeping in. I remember going to see a John Wayne film at the cinema in the late 1950's and, as kids are wont to do, came home drawling in a fake American accent. My parents were unexpectedly furious. Apparently we had not fought the war, as I had thought, to beat the Germans (although that was presumably part of it), but to keep Britain British. We had gone to all that trouble of overcoming the Axis states, only to lose our identity to a bunch of yanks. It made no sense to me then. Rock 'n' Roll was a new craze sweeping the country and driving out the incredibly dull stuff that preceded it. Fizzy drinks had arrived, and were sold in great quantities in our shop. Weekly kids' comics were brightening up the things we read and their delivery by Mr Twinn's paperboys was eagerly awaited each week. Everyone wanted to be a cowboy - even the girls. The future was bright, the future was . . . Orange County, wherever that was.

The wave of optimism that had resulted in the arrival of youngsters like me, and the surge of energy that breathed new life into a war-weary society, were waning with the realisation that the future that had been sold to the public during the hostilities was no longer on the agenda. Sure, the well-off still played croquet and went punting and the poor tended their allotments and their pigeon lofts, but something subtle had shifted. The pre-war certainties had died and the post-war future was anything but certain.

For the power brokers and the new corporate magnates, the big picture was a very different one from that of the man or woman in the street. Their future was starting to look progressively more materialist; more technologically dominated; more financially centred; more time pressured; more stressed. We kids lapped it all up - and the generation gap yawned behind us like a rift in the chronosphere. The future had arrived like an angel of deliverance, or like a bat out of hell, depending on what you were expecting - if indeed you were expecting anything.

Hamish, the would-be fighter pilot and former SAS fellow traveller, had a slightly different perspective, but one that also showed just how malleable the future can be:

> There was a lot of pride after the war that we had managed to scrape through. However, it was realised quite quickly that the European economy needed sorting out, as everyone on this side of the Atlantic was in a real mess. The news came out very soon about the lend/lease programme, whereby the US started getting new equipment into Germany to get them back on their feet, and to prevent them falling back into the economic state that was the breeding ground for fascism in the first place. So, they started rebuilding the infrastructure there. Meanwhile, what was left of our industrial base wasn't in the same league after the war. We still had this dilapidated old machinery - some of it left over from Victorian times. The Germans were getting all the brand new stuff and we weren't. I resented it. However, I came to understand that there wasn't much we could do about it, because we weren't the ones in charge of the future now. High finance and big business had taken over. It was to be the future they wanted now. We just got the crumbs.
>
> I recall that ITT was one of the armaments manufacturing companies, which had facilities that were bombed by the allies during the war. The company sued the American government for bombing their German factory - and won. They actually got reparations from their own country. I was shocked to realise that ITT had been supplying both the Germans and ourselves with ammunition. They were sitting there waiting to see who would win - and then to sue the

victors for any damages sustained from bombing. It did make me realise the underlying essence of the conflict. Of course, this other agenda only came out after the war, but it's been coming out ever since.

Along with many others, I learned the hard way that war doesn't settle anything. Because I have been fortunate enough to have been made aware, albeit for a short time, of what life is really about, and what it could be like, I'm so against people who make money from selling stuff that kills people. I really am. The world economy is dependent on the making and selling of weapons that only have one purpose - to kill people. It's an absurd situation.

It's a fundamental fault in the current world order. Our government alone is spending £76bn on refurbishing the Trident nuclear submarine system. The only thing that Trident can do is to murder millions of people and totally destroy cities. There's nothing else it can do. The argument seems to be that we won't have terrorists coming into the country if we have nuclear submarines. What use is a nuclear submarine against a terrorist? Lurking in silos all over the world are enough deteriorating nuclear bombs to destroy all human life on the planet several times over. Sabre-rattling was all very well when we were using sabres. Nothing can justify even the contemplation of using a nuclear weapon ever again.

I have a deep sorrow that we still haven't evolved enough, as a species, to realise that we don't need to settle our differences by fighting - that there are other ways of living together, that don't involve trying to dominate one another.

The Waitaha, who lived in what we now call New Zealand, came to understand the ultimate futility of war - and that was 2,000 years ago.

Despite that rant, I am actually very optimistic that we can make progress towards a more peaceful and constructive way of life, and that it could happen sooner than you might think. I know it's possible - and like anything else, if it's possible, somebody will find a way of making it happen. There have been examples of how it has come about in certain circumstances - Ghandi's India being the obvious one that comes to mind. Although he was swept away by religious and political infighting, he showed that peace can overcome fear.

If we can mobilise the majority who desperately want an end to conflict, who would prefer co-operation to competition, who have had enough of stress for stresses' sake - we could make it happen quite soon. The Management can help if we let them.

Seeing the future as just a few years of earthly life in the midst of the countless millennia of human, let alone supra-human, existence can give a very distorted perspective of what any future might hold. For those who have had the insight of an NDE, the future suddenly seems to balloon out exponentially, like a nuclear firestorm rushing away in all directions and all dimensions. For those who feel the 80-odd years of their mortal coil is the be all and end all, the world looks a very different, very much smaller place. It may be rather more comprehensible, but almost by definition, it has limited horizons.

Your place in widescreen

To make any sense of a future, let alone the sort of time-free future as pictured by Hamish, we have to stand back and look at the Big Picture. It's easier said than done. Even realising that there is a bigger picture, let alone a BIG picture is a massive mental undertaking. Assuming we can get to that starting point, finding the Big Picture can be incredibly hard in the midst of the day to day struggle to pay the mortgage, to find enough food to feed your family, or to avoid the mines of the military. Most of us are so wrapped up with getting through the day, or even the hour, that the thought of chilling out for a few weeks, or years, to contemplate the meaning of life is as close to reality as Startrek (no, sorry, that really isn't reality). Yet, if we are to evolve as individuals, as societies, or even as a species, getting the Big Picture into focus is exactly what has to happen.

Running back the video to view where we have reached to date, we see a life scattered with events of modest importance, punctuated with the odd showstopper. Did it have a direction? Should it have had one? At any point, we can stop the timeline and sense a snapshot of the period. What was the future to hold? What should we have done? A glimpse at the big picture, if we had known where to find it, would have given us a much clearer steer.

The futility of aggression, the triviality of tribalism, the sheer waste of effort spent labouring towards corporate mirages that are little more than well-marketed illusions. How could we have avoided all this dross? It's like stepping out of the stage set to discover a fast-forward world, where the houses are not just facades made of plywood. The Big Picture gives an insight into what is really going on behind the scenes in the here-and-now.

Some of us have become aware of the goal of the grail, and are creeping backwards from the screen, unimaginably slowly, to get some focus on the scale and the structure of the Big Picture - but to do so academically is a painfully protracted process in a life that flashes past.

As an only child, with no children of my own, I have had more time than most to work it through. Yet, approaching my seventh decade, I feel I have barely put one foot on the path. All those sages, who say that making the first step is the most difficult, have clearly never tried to take a second.

A few people, however - like some chap in the olden days, struck by lightning on a road to Damascus, and that other bloke who worked too hard at making a fortune in furniture and crashed out in overload - did find the Big Picture, seemingly more by luck than judgement.

You don't have to take mind-altering drugs or go bungee jumping over the Rio Grande - indeed, I would strongly counsel you against both - but you do need to be able to step back, to mentally stand outside of your self. It's so easy to say and, unless you've had a day-return to visit The Management, so very, very hard to do.

Even sensing that the Big Picture exists is such a breakthrough, which is why the outlook of so many of those who come back from an NDE is changed - fundamentally, comprehensively, irrevocably changed.

They can see where the few bits of the jigsaw that they <u>have</u> managed to accumulate fit into the picture on the front of the box. Suddenly, it all makes a little bit of sense. There is an inkling of reason; a smidgeon of logic. Hatred, fear, desire, selfishness gradually fall away - at least to the extent that such impurities can be brushed aside in the whirl of the workaday world.

While we will all see a different facet and a different aspect of the Big Picture, what we see is so much less important than the realisation that there is something to see.

In Search of the Golden Age

Much of the latter part of this book has inevitably tapped into the received wisdom of ancient knowledge. Hamish's insight at the NDE, and his subsequent revelations through dowsing, particularly in the southern hemisphere, led him to the conclusion that there is something deeply significant in this field of research. While many populist books have done much to discredit the idea that there was a time, long, long ago in the Kingdom of Zog, where everyone was happy and enlightened, HM's own direct contact with the non-physical screams at him that we should not throw out the baby of enlightenment with the murky bathwater of commercial fiction.

So the time had come for a BIG question - and it was met with the longest and most pregnant pause of the whole project. I asked him if he felt there had ever been a 'Golden Age'. After a very long rumination, he ventured:

> I think there have been a number of Golden Ages. Every one possibly failed because of the human need for survival, which creates aggression. In this Great Life Cycle, we have been developing our technical abilities, but we have failed to realise, so far, that the aggression we needed for survival in the days of the sabre-toothed tiger, we don't need any more. We've reached a point where aggression is no longer necessary, but it is so inbred in this particular species that we are finding it incredibly difficult to breed it out.

> We are still expressing the need for survival by imposing our will on other people. The whole world economy is based on domination and aggression, rather than love - and that is the source of 90% of our problems. We haven't yet grasped that we don't need the aggression any more; that we've got beyond it; that our entire survival does not depend on the size of our club, so that we can beat up the tiger. If we are to have a future of any value, and I am sure that we will have at some point, then we have to recognise and relegate this base aggression.

I don't feel that Golden Ages are geared to physical conditions; they are geared to the human ability to work with the natural environment, in its broadest sense.

If we had a group living around here in Trencrom, where each person had different skills, abilities and insights - and we were able to pool those resources to help one another - that would produce a Golden Age in Trencrom.

It's very, very simple. I think that's the type of society that we have to try to evolve - and I think it's quite possible, if only we can take a longer view and a wider perspective.

I'm not suggesting that we have to go and live in tepees - not that I have anything against people who choose that route - but we need to develop groups of people with different talents, who each contribute to a way of life that is less stressful.

As a culture we have created our own stress - even members of my own family have a stressful way of life that seems to be very much of their own making. Alternative ways of living just don't seem to occur to them. We have invented and enforced material living standards on ourselves that are just impossible to sustain - and we are suffering for it in non-physical ways.

Yes, there have been Golden Ages, but I don't think they have happened in a particular tribe at a particular time. I think they have come to pass inside small, contented groups of people - like the Kogi (in South America), who call us the 'little brothers' because we don't seem to understand the basics. We're destroying our own planet - and they can see it being destroyed all around them.

I'm not suggesting that we could all live off the land and sit around meditating - although that might be a good start - and I'm only too aware that a lot people reading this book will be thinking 'It's all right for him living in a beautiful part of Cornwall, but it's very different if you live in a high-rise flat'.

But, if I have been able to do anything useful with my life, that you can pass on to others through this book, it's that I have been able to prize open a few doors - just a little. I hope I have been able to demonstrate that it is possible to develop a different way of thinking and living in this cycle, and that can set you off on a more positive path for the long haul.

An alternative to religion

Hamish came from that solid tradition of post-war thinkers, who could make no sense of the religion that had been thrown at them in their youth - with the result that they understandably ignored it. I am even in danger here of giving the prevailing official belief too high a status, because people like the pre-NDE Hamish felt there was so little substance in the subject, there was nothing to ignore. Like most of us, he might join in with a Christmas carol after a few drams, but that was about it.

To the last, Hamish never had much time for ceremony and solemnity. He saw the mediaeval meanderings and the histrionic hierarchies of the major faiths as just so much social posturing. Yet, as we have seen, the post-NDE Hamish was obliged to take a long hard look at a world that for the young businessman just didn't exist. While some who have been through the NDE have re-found their own cultural religious heritage, for Hamish it was a completely unexpected journey into a virgin dimension.

That said, as he has recounted his NDE experience and his subsequent revelations, it became clear that much of what he had come to accept didn't actually conflict with the essence of the early philosophies. In particular, many of those emanating from the eastern hemisphere would fit comfortably alongside the 21st Century Millerworld, which was still under construction at the time of his passing over.

His insights into 'the cycle of life', 'the role of karma', 'the evolution of the soul', 'the re-evaluation at the entrance to the otherworld', 'the spark of the divine in all of us' could easily be rebadged into one or other of the major religions. Above The Management, he felt there was layer upon layer of ever more highly evolved entities, perhaps even reaching up to some incomprehensible source of creation, with which it could be our ultimate destiny to merge. There wasn't much there to frighten the horses of the theologically inclined.

However, Hamish had no time for the culture of the cult; he was desperate not to spark off yet another cult - however well intentioned - and he certainly didn't want the posthumous status of cultural icon. However, he did have a burning desire to explain what he felt he had been privileged to discover - and for that insight to be made available to others who were to follow.

He was irrepressibly optimistic and enthusiastic that his enlightenment really could provide an opportunity for a redefined understanding of the meaning of life itself.

Quite an ambition for someone who still saw himself as just an 'ordinary bloke'.

No freewheeling

At the time of writing, Hamish had been given a limited medical life - long enough to sort himself out and engage the launch position, but not long enough to embark on anything major.

So, when we came to discuss his understanding and his intuition of the way ahead, I had expected him to launch into a magical mystery tour of myth and legend made manifest. Instead, his first priority was to tidy up his affairs, so that Ba would not be left with a mess to sort out on her own.

In latter months, standing stones that had been lying about for decades, waiting to be erected in the garden, were stood up. Equipment that had been in desperate need of replacement for years was replaced. Moves were even afoot to update his autobiography!

It was very difficult to envisage Hamish ever easing up. He declared that 2009 was to have been a sabbatical year; a year where he took his foot off the accelerator, stopped doing talks and presentations for a while, and didn't take up any new initiatives.

Yet, while we were researching this work, each time I visited Treviscoe, people came to the door, usually unexpectedly, in a steady stream. He was on the receiving end of so many phone calls that eventually he was obliged to pull the plug out of the wall to give us a little breathing space. It wore me out, and it wasn't even my life.

He was dedicated to giving The Parallel Community a push-start; he loved holding his dowsing workshops; he understood the importance of making presentations about what he had discovered; he drew great strength from debating with his friends and in rekindling his family bonds. If you take pleasure and pride in what you do, it's not work.

Despite his enlightened and thoughtful approach to life, Hamish never became vague or detached. He was as driven in his eighties, perhaps even more so, than when he was rushing around the world selling metal chairs. There were so many exciting things to sense and experience, so many avenues still to investigate, yet so little sand left in the egg-timer. It was just part of his baggage - and I was sure it would be something he would carry with him when he boarded the next flight.

The Creation of Reality

Coming to terms with reality

What is reality, exactly? Answers on a postcard, please.

One of the essential themes that emerged from Hamish's work, and will doubtless be carried forward by others, is the idea that reality is not a given; not a hard and fast set of external rules; not a solid, impenetrable lump. It is as malleable as the imagination and consciousness of the viewer.

It can be argued that Hamish was hardly alone in this assertion, but through his NDE and his application of dowsing to the idea, he has given the concept a vigorous new impetus.

In the last quarter of the last century, a whole new industry sprang up with the stated aim of modifying reality. People who were unhappy, or out of kilter, with their current position or their previous outlook could turn to a new breed of professional. These gurus would show them that they were (a) not alone and (b) just a blink away from being satisfied and fulfilled. The life coach was born.

For some decades the coaching of various disciplines had been starting to show that the reality you thought you were stuck with, was anything but. Sportsmen and women in particular had been adding mental skills and awareness to physical prowess and dexterity. No-hope teams were given hope. Losers were shown that their position was, at least in part, of their own making and could be turned around. Having belief in yourself really could make you into someone else. The structural framework remains much the same, but the way you work with it changes.

Some of this work can be as simple as the old trick of persuading the client that 'their glass is half full, rather than half empty'. Even that can be a huge step forward, but there are far more profound undercurrents to tap into.

The life coach takes the narrowly focused sporting approach and gives it a more holistic makeover. Many people have been able to sort out their lives with the assistance of such people. As any life coach reading these lines will tell you, the client has to sort themselves out - the coach only provides the space, the potential and the sounding board that leads the client to understand why they are where they are - and that there really are alternative options open to them. Many of these options may involve jettisoning comfort blankets from the past, but in essence, the only thing that ties you to this current, lacklustre reality - is yourself.

There is nothing particularly spiritual about this process, but it does show that reality is, to some extent at least, what you make it.

In one of my previous jobs, I managed to acquire the role of Redundancy Councillor. I was sent on a course, somewhere in the Midlands, at which we had a couple of days of training on how to be nice to people who were about to lose their life-long employment for the benefit of the stock market, and how to do our best to give them a bit of help and hope. It was very valuable actually, but the precise content of the course is not relevant here. What was significant was the get-to-know-you session at the start. The tutor merely asked us to note down who we were and what we did - and what we would like to do with our lives if there were no external factors stopping us. Needless to say, we all commented that we would like to be writers, painters, travellers or philosophers rather than personnel officers. Having patiently heard our contributions, the tutor then asked us, in a matter-of-fact sort of way, what the hell we were doing there and why were we not somewhere else, pursuing our dreams. For a few minutes there was a corporate howl of protest about responsibilities for children, the need to pay mortgages and a lack of personal skills. Gradually, however, it died down, and by lunchtime we really were left thinking what on earth <u>were</u> we doing there! Even asking the question was such a powerful exercise that our realities changed a little. I am sure it helped each of us to help others in the years ahead - and quite bizarrely, in my case, set me off on a road that did indeed result in my having the courage to change my career.

But all this, constructive and demonstrative though it may be, is superficial compared to the older traditions on which it stands. It is a common theme of most of the Buddhist schools that all of life is an illusion. Think about that for a few seconds! I have always found this to be a wonderfully empowering outlook, but I feel, as with so much of the wisdom that has percolated across the globe from the east, some of the meaning has been lost in translation. It is not that the world around us does not exist - it is a real phenomenon in four dimensional space and time (oh, yes it is). Where the eastern tradition does bring ancient knowledge to bear on the modern world is in appreciating that with infinite energy, possibly uncountable lives and boundless opportunities, our reality really is what we make of it. What the eastern awareness brings to the table, and the likes of Hamish Miller tapped into, is that awareness can be expanded exponentially. To do so at a stroke would probably be too much for any entity to handle, but to work towards it through a lifetime, or many lifetimes, seems more credible.

The tradition that Hamish discovered, via Barry Brailsford in New Zealand, added further dimensions to this debate. The reality of the first inhabitants of the southern islands, the Waitaha, appeared to differ from those of us with a western worldview in several fundamental ways.

Primarily, we see ourselves as distinct entities, separated from all others around us - and indeed, we consider all other entities to be separated from each other. The Waitaha felt all people, animals, plants and even elements of what we would term 'the mineral kingdom' were part of a continuous undulating flow of energy.

The Waitaha also seemed to experience a radically different reality of time. To them, the past, and possibly the future, were felt to have much the same quality as the present. Events that occurred in the history of the culture were considered to be as current that day, and as relevant now as when they had happened chronologically, decades or even centuries earlier.

Wisdom of the Waitaha

In a similar vein to an increasing number of western sensitives, the Waitaha were acutely aware of the 'energy of place'. They seemed to be almost as conscious of the energy profile of a location as the visual spectrum. Their apparent ability to work with the energy of the place would have provided them with a very different view of the malleability of familiar locations and everyday artefacts. It could even be that they saw nothing as inherently fixed - and even the very concept of reality, as we would describe it, might have been almost an alien idea.

> Sadly, the remaining Waitaha don't practise this at all, but their forefathers had an amazing degree of concentration that we can't even begin to understand. Unless you have that degree of concentration, you can't create a reality - you may be able to alter a reality under certain circumstances, but you wouldn't be able to create it.
>
> The Waitaha had a special method of selecting youngsters, who had a propensity to take on board the knowledge of the

stars, the skills of navigation, knowledge of the sea shore, growing food, the lore of the forests, the use of stone . . . of bringing on the responsive children who could control their anger. They realised that this was one of the most important qualities; ensuring that those who were chosen to take on these skills weren't diverted by anger.

They recorded their group memories in song and passed them down for a thousand years. The memory training was so intense that the stories were allegedly still being recited word perfect after many generations. One of these stories is of a Waitaha girl, who was trained from the age of five. In her mid-twenties she was allowed to move up to the highest level of tuition, where she was taught one-to-one with one of the tohunga, one of the great teachers. Her particular skill was that she could sit on top of a 100ft cliff and tune into a single shell on the shore - after it had been covered by the tide! That's a degree of concentration that we can't begin to comprehend.

Most of the men were murdered 700 years ago by a very belligerent crowd of invaders. However, many of the women of that time survived and vowed to keep their culture alive by committing the Waitaha songs to memory. There is a folk-memory amongst the survivors that, at some point in time, the details of their wonderful way of life will be released - and that there will then be a perfect recitation of everything about the Waitaha culture. When Barry (Brailsford) came to write his book, he found they had a shortened version of their history, which was still orally recorded in over 3,000 songs! Although it was a different type of history to what we are accustomed to in the West, there is little doubt about the type of Waitaha culture that actually existed.

Having discussed it at great length with Barry - and considered it in the light of what I have experienced and discovered for myself - I am drawn to believe that the Waitaha may well have been capable of manifesting their reality and, under certain exceptional circumstances, even bringing it into physical form.

Creating our own reality?

Just as we need to create a reality for ourselves, to make some sense of this particular time and place, so it seems that we need to do so to comprehend the even more difficult-to-understand realms that may lie beyond it.

We saw in a previous chapter that different people have different ways of expressing their NDE - and that, understandably, they tend to use a language and an iconography that is meaningful to them. Christians use Christian terminology, Hindus use Hindu terminology - and Hamish Miller found a bunch of blokes sitting around a grid control panel, flicking levers and altering the frequencies of energy lines. A bit irreverent I accept, but I am sure he would have acknowledged that it is very much the sense of his experience. An ancient Egyptian, an Aztec sun god worshipper, a member of the 19th century Wee Free Church and a furniture designer in 20th century Sussex would all have to express their views verbally and pictorially in the only way they would know how. They had to create the reality they experienced as they saw it. A Roman legionary would see a run-of-the-mill motorbike as a terrifying horseless chariot, and a biker today would see a run-of-the-mill interplanetary shuttle service from the Andromeda galaxy as a mindblowing UFO.

As we have seen, Hamish's personal experience led him to the understanding, the take on reality, that the individual 'soul' continues through countless cycles, developing towards a higher evolutionary state. The process is technically called Transmigration. My own trail of thought has led me over many decades - but without any direct spiritual experience - to the view that at the end of this life, the energy that is within us drops back into the greater pool of life, ready for a more corporate form of recycling. This is a process known as Transcendence - but then again, that's just my current reality!

If we do indeed create our own reality, even of something as personally tangible as an out of body experience, is anything real at all? I certainly agree with Hamish in finding the concept of an individually framed future a 'wonderfully liberating idea'.

The fear of letting go - of fear

NDE returners like Hamish are left with a bewildering new set of choices. For many, it is as much as they can handle to shoehorn their strange experience into the world they thought they understood - to live out a life of patient acceptance in constructive contentment. Others feel morally obliged to take the hardest road, that of the evangelist, spreading the good news that they have chanced upon, and couching it in the language of their time and station. Some become the movers and shakers of the positively radical, regardless of - or perhaps because of - their former existence. They can grow into activists, campaigners, healers, benefactors, Good Samaritans, maybe even founders of movements such as the Parallel Community.

The NDE bestows on the involuntary traveller the realisation that most of what we temporary mortals fear - and therefore what we fight hardest to avoid or to overcome - is actually little more than an illusion. Fear is yet another part of our self-inflicted reality that manifests itself in many subtle ways - hatred, prejudice, pride, the need to control, the lack of self-confidence . . . Viewed from the dimension visited by the NDE survivor, the opaque becomes transparent; the watertight, permeable; fear, little more than a myopic mirage.

It is often said that 'money is the root of all evil'. However, it is not the use of usury in itself that hobbles us; it is the desire for wealth that sits at the heart of our present dilemma. Desire draws us into the whirlpool of anguish that leads us to fight to retain what we have, and to covet the oxen of others. Yet even the reduction of desire, which is so central to the mantras of the venerable eastern philosophies, is itself not our problem at its basest level.

Understandably, we seek wealth, material security and status to assuage our fear of poverty, insecurity and worthlessness. However, having overcome these basic needs, we carry on desiring, accumulating and struggling. Like a pendulum that has forgotten to swing back, we pursue our direction long after the original stimulus has ceased. We fear what might conceivably happen in some vaguely possible future set of circumstances. Fear seems almost innate.

Again and again in my discussions with Hamish, I heard him voice the refrain 'no fear'. After the NDE, for him fear had all but ceased to exist. It's so much easier to say than to embody, but in his presence you could faintly feel that freedom from fear. Not a Braveheart fearlessness, not a cavalier fearhardiness, just a subtle awareness of the absence of fear.

> The biggest change the NDE made to my life was the realisation that fear need have no part to play. It's an illusion we have constructed for ourselves. It's a prison of our own making. If I could convey one thing of my experience to anyone who might read this book, it is the importance of letting go of fear.

In the absence of fear, there is just love.

The Miller Legacy

This book has chronicled the life - or, more accurately, the lives - of Hamish Miller; designer and businessman turned dowser, healer, philosopher and activist. It was intended to read as just a story of the life of a man - albeit a rather exceptional man - but it has become so much more than that.

In amongst the events and the anecdotes, there was a series of discoveries and rediscoveries, ideas, hypotheses and flashes of inspiration, which were born out of his personal experience. With the passing of time and the absorption of some of these ideas into the mainstream of Alternative Theory, it will become all too easy to underestimate the contribution that these insights have made to the evolution of human thought, and to our understanding of the world we are moving through.

I hesitate to call this chapter an Executive Summary, as that would seem incompatible with the flowing spirit of this particular journey. However, it is important, especially for all those reading this text in years to come, to appreciate that these are some of the ideas that Hamish brought - or brought back - into focus.

Earth Energy
Natural centres and lines of force that may encircle the earth and can be found almost everywhere. They have been 'dowsed' by men and women throughout recorded history and, based on the evidence from pre-historic stone structures, way back into the mists of time. Energy lines and energy centres can be detected with inexpensive devices like homemade rods or a pendulum. Earth Energy is essentially beneficial, uplifting and health-promoting and adds meaning to many of the natural and man-made features in the landscape.

Pictograms in the Ether
Patterns, symbols and icons that are described in Earth Energy at significant (and possibly other) places. The meaning and derivation of these enigmatic diagrams is unclear, but they seem to be patterns created by natural earth energies interacting with the consciousness of the dowser. They may be related to similar, more complex, graphical displays found in other media, such as certain crop circles.

Manifestations at Nodal Points
Organic patterns, usually geometrical in shape, which form at the
crossing points of major Earth Energy networks. These appear to retain
their form throughout the length of significant energy lines, but morph
over time in response to the intent and attention of the dowser.

The Earth Communicates
Becoming aware, through the sensing of changes in the response of Earth
Energy to the presence and intent of the dowser, that the planet is a living
entity in its own right, in addition to being the sum of its parts (of which
we are just one element).

The Value of Healing
A process of promoting and fostering improved physical, mental,
emotional and spiritual health - without any direct physical intervention.
This highly effective and quietly widespread practice usually uses
'channelled' healing energy from an external source. The realisation that
healing the land is at least as important as healing the individual.

The Near Death Experience (NDE)
The sensation of moving out of the physical body and passing on to
another plane, whilst being in full possession of all conscious faculties -
and with an extended awareness of memory. An astonishingly
widespread, well-researched and well-documented phenomenon.

The Management
An awareness that human beings can evolve into a heightened spiritual
state, subtly linked to, but not directly connected with, the world we
inhabit today. The Management may have the ability and the desire to
aid humanity, but need our practical assistance to enable 'them' to
influence the course of events.

The Parallel Community
A pioneering organisation that seeks to bond like-minded groups
together; to give heart to those of an enlightened nature; to counter the
destructive power of those who would seek to gain excessive advantage
within one cycle; to offer hope for a more constructive and less
materialist world.

The cycle of life

An appreciation that we come into this dimension to learn and to contribute; we do what we can for the planet as a whole and for those around us; we move on and maybe, in due course, move up.

The nature of spirits

The understanding that most spirits are just people who no longer have bodies; that they are stuck in a lonely and confused existence and, in many cases, need some help to move on.

The Big Picture

The ability to stand back and see your own construct of reality as it really is. This is not the local and fairly inconsequential bit you have felt it necessary to stare at up to now, but the BIG PICTURE, of which you are a tiny, yet highly significant, pixel.

The Creation of Reality

The appreciation that we all have the ability to shape the way we see our own lives and that 'reality' is not completely fixed. Certain cultures, at certain windows in their history, may have had the ability to create their own awareness and their own destiny more clearly than we can at present. However, with hard work and intent, this could happen again in this dimension through enlightened evolution.

The Illusion of Fear

Without fear, the world is a very different place. As John Lennon might once have said, imagine - no desire for property beyond personal needs, no inclination to selfishness, no tendency to hate, no tribes, no countries, no religions, no separation, nothing to fight or die for - I wonder if you can?

Seizing the Moment

While it may not be unique to Hamish, one of the most impressive themes that recurred throughout his life was the ability to see and to seize opportunities. While one might connect such awareness with the young entrepreneur, it was also an ability that he was able to tap into with great vigour during his post-NDE years. Arguably, Hamish was presented with more chances than most to expand his horizons, but the frequency with which he realised and capitalised on the possibility of the half-chance is a lesson to us all. It's a hackneyed cliché, but nonetheless a very important one - Make Every Day Count.

The value of laughter

In the first draft of the text of this book, I left in the transcripts of Hamish's spoken words all of the times that he laughed aloud during our discussions - at events, at situations, but mostly at himself. In the final draft, I took out most of these references, as they were so numerous they might have seemed irritating to many readers who had never actually met the man.

When we started this project, I thought it would essentially be a much grander version of the academic event write-ups for which I am more widely known in dowsing circles. What actually transpired were many months of pure joy, repeatedly punctuated by Hamish's infectious and very genuine laughter.

HM never lost sight of the gravity and importance of his work, nor of the significance of the path he was on, but equally he never let the world get him down. He laughed at those twists of fate that left him bewildered, penniless and looking distinctly silly - and he laughed at his most momentous failures. For me, it has been an object lesson in how to take life seriously, without ever lapsing into sanctimony.

Despite spending fifty-odd years in a strictly secular frame of mind, Hamish became aware that he was being guided, by forces unknown, to be in certain places, at certain times and in a particular sequence. Some of these events or confluences could clearly have been co-incidences in the traditional sense of the word, but as a coherent series they seemed to add up to something more profound - somewhere between intuition and induction.

His intention in asking me to compile this book was not in any way to enlarge his already iconic status. I can vouch for the fact that he had precious little interest in such matters and derived no satisfaction from them. What he did want to convey was a greater understanding of the vast, unexplored realms that lie beyond the five gross senses. Perhaps more importantly, and certainly most urgently, he strongly encouraged us to start, each in our own small way, to use that awareness to turn the world away from its current perilous social and spiritual trajectory.

Hamish never claimed to have discovered or invented anything entirely by himself - other than four engineering patents for 'mechanical constructions' that he had to his name. He freely acknowledged that, like every other thinker and researcher of note before him, he 'stood on the shoulders of giants'. In turn, he desperately wanted those who were to follow after him to learn from <u>his</u> experience. He encouraged us - no, he incited us - to pick up the baton he was handed so unexpectedly, and to run with it, as if our reality depended on it.

It was both a great privilege and a great pleasure to have been asked to assist him in this endeavour.

Hamish Miller - Blacksmith and Sculptor

As we have seen, from a very young age, Hamish was fascinated with the alchemy of the Blacksmith - the process of taking lumps of base metal, applying fire, water and air and producing useful objects and works of art.

It was his boyhood dream, and one that was an ever-present element of his life - right up to his last few days.

He always felt that his better-known revelations were, in some fashion, passed to him from external sources. His role was to make sense of them, develop the themes and pass them on to the next generation. The art of the Blacksmith was something else. It was just himself and his tools - creating something wonderful, seemingly out of the ether.

Given the extraordinary events of his life, it was vital for Hamish to be able to keep a least one foot in the here and now, or he could so easily have become yet another otherworldly dreamer drifting through life, imparting little value.

While I try to keep grounded by digging the good soil of Devon or rambling the less well-known parts of Dartmoor, for Hamish the 'real' world was the time he spent in his forge. In a strange way, I feel his personal mastery of this ancient skill is actually how he would like to be remembered by posterity.

I am no art critic, and certainly no artist, so I will simply end this book with illustrations of the produce of his hammer and anvil - which speak for themselves.

Suggested Further Reading and Viewing

Hamish Miller - published works

Hamish Miller
> It's Not Too Late — Penwith Press
> The Definitive Wee Little Book of Dowsing — Penwith Press
> A Journey Beyond the Five Senses — Wooden Books

Hamish Miller & Paul Broadhurst
> The Sun and the Serpent — Pendragon Press
> The Dance of the Dragon — Pendragon Press
> (with Ba Russell and Vivienne Shanley)
> Maps of the routes of these two projects — Penwith Press

Hamish Miller & Barry Brailsford
> In Search of the Southern Serpent — Stoneprint Press
> Penwith Press — Website

Works inspired by the above

Frances Lewis and Adelina Abad Pedrosa
> Name of book to be announced — Publisher to be announced

Jane Bottomley et al
> Awakening Albion — Edge of Time

Dowsing - General

Sig Lonegren
> Spiritual Dowsing — Gothic Image

Tom Graves
> Needles of Stone — Grey House in the Woods

John Michell
> The View over Atlantis — Abacus
> City of Revelation — Abacus
> The Old Stones of Land's End — Unknown

Guy Underwood
> Pattern of the Past — Abacus

Alan Neal
> Dowsing in Devon and Cornwall — Bossiney

W A (Billy) Gawn
> Megalithic Structures - why? — W.A. Gawn

Sheila Ostrander and Lynn Schroeder
> PSI: Psychic Discoveries Behind the Iron Curtain — Abacus

Ley Lines

Alfred Watkins
> The Old Straight Track — Abacus
> The Ley Hunter's Manual — Turnstone Press

Crop Circles
Freddy Silva
        Secrets in the Fields   Hampton Roads
Steve and Karen Alexander (Temporary Temples)   Website
Lucy Pringle   Website

Healing
Barbara Brennan
        Hands of Light   Bantam
Lyall Watson
        Supernature: A Natural History of the Supernatural Sceptre
Masaru Emoto
        Hidden Messages in Water   HADO Kyoikusha
                                                       Website
Colin Bloy
        Dowsing the Dragon   Fountain International
E H Shattock
        A Manual of Self-healing   Turnstone Press
        Mind your Body   Turnstone Press
Jude Currivan
        The Wave   O Books

Near Death Experiences
P M H Atwater
        The Big Book of Near Death Experiences   Hampton Roads
Raymond Moody
        Life After Life   Harper
Deepak Chopra
        Life After Death   Rider

International Association for Near Death Studies (IANDS) Website

DVDs
Spirit of the Serpent   Knights Rose
Diverse Dowsing   TWA Associates
Hamish on the Parallel Community   TWA Associates
Moments of Peace (interview)   Knights Rose
The Day I Died   BBC

Video
Erdenlicht   Pegasus Film Trucking

The British Society of Dowsers can be contacted at:

4/5 Cygnet Centre,
Worcester Road,
Hanley Swan,
Worcestershire
WR8 0EA
Tel +44 (0)1684 576969.

Email: info@britishdowsers.org

Website: www.britishdowsers.org

The Code of Ethical Conduct of The British Society of Dowsers

1. Dowsing Wisely

In your dowsing generally, and when people seek your assistance as a dowser, keep your dowsing focussed on issues of genuine need. Recognise and work within the limits of your competence, and refer to another practitioner or other source if necessary.

2. Dowsing with Respect

Only dowse for information that concerns you personally or that lies within an area of public concern, unless you are asked or given permission by other people to dowse either for them personally or for groups or organisations of which they are members. Do not dowse for information about other people or their concerns without their permission, unless it is clearly in the interest of the highest common good to do so, and do not make unsolicited comments about other people or their concerns based on your dowsing.

Always treat people requesting information about dowsing or who ask you to dowse politely and considerately. When dowsing for others, respect their views, their dignity and their privacy, and protect personal or confidential information of which you may become aware. Explain what you are doing, give your conclusions and advice in a manner that they can understand, and respect their right to consent to or to decline what you offer or advise.

Make sure that your personal beliefs do not prejudice your interactions with other people when you are dowsing, or with the people for whom you dowse - you must not allow your views about anyone's lifestyle, culture, belief, race, colour, gender, sexuality, age, social status or perceived economic worth to prejudice your dowsing.

3. Trustworthy Dowsing

Honest and trustworthy behaviour is expected from every dowser, and it is most important that you avoid abusing your position as a dowser.

Be careful not to use your position as a dowser to create or establish improper relationships, either personal or financial. Never misuse privileged information that you may obtain through dowsing. If people seek your assistance as a dowser, be careful to use your dowsing only for their genuine benefit, give guidance and recommendations that you believe to be in their best interests, and share with them all relevant information that you may discover.

4. Providing Information About Dowsing

When providing information about dowsing, it must be factual and verifiable. Avoid sensational or misleading statements, and be mindful of the likely accuracy and completeness of your dowsing as well as of the effects that your information may have on other people as well as on public opinion generally. If dowsing for health or therapies of any kind, you must not offer guarantees of cures, nor exploit people's vulnerability or lack of knowledge, nor put pressure on people to use a service, for example by arousing fear for their future health or well-being. You must not make claims about the comparative quality of your dowsing nor compare your abilities with those of other dowsers.

5. Respecting Relationships With Other Dowsers

Be open and fair with other dowsers, and be willing to consult with them. You must never discriminate unfairly against other dowsers, or allow your views of their lifestyle, culture, belief, race, colour, gender, sexuality, age, or social status to prejudice your relationship with them.

You must not make anyone doubt another dowser's knowledge or skills by making unnecessary or unsustainable comments about them.

6. Financial & Commercial Dealings

You must be honest in any financial and commercial matters relating to your dowsing practice. If you are receiving money for your dowsing you must inform people of all costs before you begin, and you must declare any personal commercial interest in goods or services that you recommend.

7. Legal Issues

You must observe any laws that affect your dowsing and obtain adequate insurance for any aspects of your dowsing practice that requires it.

8. Teaching & Training

The BSD encourages you to continually improve your dowsing knowledge and skills, to help the public to be aware of and understand dowsing, and to contribute to the education and training of other dowsers. Please see details about the BSD training programme.

9. The British Society of Dowsers

The British Society of Dowsers exists to provide a forum for dowsers to meet and exchange ideas and experiences, to support and promote good and responsible dowsing, and to provide information about dowsing and dowsers. The BSD Office is always happy to receive calls from dowsers and from members of the public with dowsing related enquiries. We hope that you will support the Society, participate in our events, contribute to the Journal, and enjoy a long and fruitful membership with us.

The Parallel Community can be contacted at:

The Parallel Community
PO Box 11
Hayle
Cornwall UK
TR27 6YF

Email: parallelcommunity@hotmail.co.uk

Website: www.parallelcommunity.com

Aims of The Parallel Community

1. To inaugurate a 'parallel community' programme with which people who are concerned about current global thinking on economic and political matters can identify, and through which they can make their own positive contribution towards solutions.

2. To establish that we as human beings have the absolute right to live in peace not only with our neighbours but with everyone on this earth, and to formally claim that right.

3. To re-establish our natural rapport with all other beings on the planet and in the cosmos.

4. To acknowledge our collective responsibility to care for, have compassion for, and love our fellow humans, recognising that while we have amongst us a plethora of belief systems, we must respect these differences and move beyond them.

5. To understand that many hundreds of thousands of people in discussion in small groups feel exactly as we do, and while at the moment there is no effective platform to express our collective distress, we must make use of modern technology to bring our aims to the notice of all such people so that we can perhaps combine to make our voices heard.

6. To present a non-confrontational alternative to the decision-making systems which are currently destroying our quality of life and ultimately our precious planet.

7. To establish that political decisions at any level based on war and killing fellow humans as a solution to global and local problems are no longer acceptable in the 21st century. We recognise that we cannot change the nature of current warmongers, and must have compassion for them as degenerates, but we need not and will not blindly accept their destructive decisions as we have done for generations.

8. To start in a small way in our own communities with the simple gestures of a smile and a helping hand for anyone we feel might need a lift.

9. To rebuild honest communications systems independent of 'spin'.

10. To provide a tangible message of hope for people who have lost their identity, their sense of wonder at the marvels of nature, and their ability to laugh in the pure enjoyment of living.

11. To establish a website so that people can join the parallel community.

12. To use the massive energy available in human minds to make a difference to our future.

Fountain International can be contacted at:

Joy Byner
Fountain International Co-ordinator
20 Hickstead Park,
Hassocks,
Sussex BN6 9HR
United Kingdom

Email: terry.monnery@ukonline.co.uk

Website: www.fountain-international.org

Extract from The Alphega Manifesto (1986):

We, the peoples of the planet, do hereby solemnly declare
that among the rights that are variously attributed to
human beings, one right is paramount and that is the right to live for the indefinite
future in a safe and unpolluted environment, whether threats to that environment
come from spiritual, chemical or nuclear origins.

We further declare that whereas certain human rights are well specified, if not
always well satisfied, no such attribution of human duties resides in any formal
statement, to which individuals may look for guidance. . . .

. . . The time has come to call a halt, and for the voice and aspirations of ordinary
people across the world to make itself irresistible, and to require those people in
the systems and institutions that make the decisions that affect their future, to be
beholden to their duties for humanity. . . .

. . . Thus we call upon the governments of the world to abandon once and for
always the use of nuclear energy . . . and to replace it with other forms of energy
that does not represent the same threat to mankind. . . .

. . . We further call for the immediate imposition of controls on the emission of
effluent of a chemical nature into the environment . . .

. . . It is simply the voice of humanity demanding the right of survival from those
who have the duty to provide it . . .

. . . behind The Fountain Group lies a deep understanding that man's
responsibility to his neighbour is enshrined in the concept of love and duty,
whatever his religion or ideology, without which the world will not survive, and
thus it can threaten no state, no ideology, no religion, no structure or institution or
individual, save those who do not henceforth recognise their environmental duty
to their neighbour and their planet.

Colin Bloy 19.6.86

About Fountain International

Fountain is a world-wide community healing project based on the simple concept that communities, like people, suffer from dis-ease, and may be healed. By tuning-in one's thoughts to an agreed point of focus in one's own community for just a few moments of each day, it is possible to radically improve the health of the community, and ultimately, we believe, the health of the world.

Fountain Groups are so called because of the first one, which was formed in Brighton (UK) in 1981 using a beautiful fountain as its focal point or *Hara*. The fountain, in the Old Steine, is well known and positioned on a main 'ley line', on what may be called the spinal column of the town. It also marks the centre of an old stone circle commemorated in the name 'Old Steine', the ancient megaliths of which are in the base of the fountain.

Fountain is open to EVERYONE, of whatever faith, colour, nationality or political persuasion. There is no membership or organisation in the usual sense, and all the individuals or groups throughout the world work independently in the manner best suited to their own communities. However, they do this with the feeling of being a part of a network, and the thought that group activity produces an effect greater than the sum of the parts.

All that is required (apart from the genuine desire to do something positive to improve conditions in the community) is the commitment to devote just 2 or 3 minutes a day linking in thought to an agreed *Hara* within the community. This might be a village cross, church spire, memorial or other well known landmark.

After stilling the mind, the focal point is visualised radiating healing energy (Light and Love) throughout the community. This may be done on your own at home, however, it is also good to meet as a group with like-minded friends from time to time. The group may then tune in to the *Hara* or any part of the community requiring extra help and carry out this Fountain meditation. Afterwards the group may discuss results and changes occurring throughout the community.

Significant events in the life of Hamish Miller

1927	Born in Bo'ness, West Lothian, Scotland
1932-39	Bo'ness Public School and Bo'ness Academy
1939-44	George Heriot's School, Edinburgh.
1942	Out of body experience - The Cobbler
1942-44	St. Andrew's University
1944-46	National Service Training with Commandos firstly SAS group, then RE (Deputy Military Mechanist, Electrical - Corporal)
1946-48	Heriot Watt University
1949	GEC Scotland - Edinburgh and Glasgow (Illuminating Engineer)
1953	GEC London - lighting fittings designer
1953	First marriage
1954	First son, Roderick, born
1954	Small Workshop in Twickenham - one employee
1955	Moved to West Sussex. Small factory in Findon - 6 employees. Larger factory in Steyning - 8 employees.
1957	Built factory in Smalldole, Sussex. Expanded furniture business.
1960	Second marriage
1962	Second son, Sean, born
1973	Bought land near Hayle, Cornwall
1978	Sinking of the fishing boat, *Hopeful*
1982	Near Death Experience - UK
Late 1982	Closure of furniture business. Involvement with the Fountain Group. Moved to Cornwall
Early 1983	Rented forge. Met Colin Bloy. Met Mike Colmer.

1983	Involvement with dowsing and joined the British Society of Dowers
1983	One Man, One Earth - first film project
1984-89	The Sun and the Serpent project
	Extensive ground clearance and tree planting at Treviscoe
1986	Fountain Group - Andorra
1989	*The Sun and the Serpent* published
1990 <	Development of blacksmithing
1991-99	Dance of the Dragon project
1998	*It's Not Too Late* published
2000	*Dance of the Dragon* published
2002	*The Definitive Wee Book of Dowsing* published
2002-06	Visits to America (lecturing); South America and South Africa (researching); Australia and New Zealand - In Search of the Southern Serpent project
2003	DVD *The Spirit of the Serpent*
2003-10	Erection of the Stone Circle and associated sculptures at Treviscoe
2005	Near Death Experience - Australian Hospital
2005	Third marriage
2006	*In Search of the Southern Serpent* published
2006	Inauguration of the Parallel Community
2007	DVD *Hamish on The Parallel Community*
2008	DVD *Diverse Dowsing*
2009-10	A Life Divined project

January 2010. The day after Hamish died, once the news started to circulate, the Parallel Community Website received over 47,000 separate visitors. It is a testimony to the impact he had on all those who met him - and on those he reached through his work.

Obituary - as it appeared in the local and national press in February 2010

Hamish Miller

Cornwall-based Author, Dowser, Philosopher, Activist, Blacksmith

Hamish Miller, one of Britain's best known, most highly respected and certainly best-loved dowsers, has died at his home near Lelant in Cornwall aged 82.

He was born in Bo'ness, Scotland, in 1927, the son of a dentist. In the 1940's, he attended St Andrew's and Edinburgh Universities and subsequently started his own furniture manufacturing company in Sussex. By the early 1980's, he had become a highly successful businessman, but in 1982 he suffered complications during a major abdominal operation and effectively died on the operating table. The Near Death Experience (NDE), with which he later came to terms, changed the course his life radically and irrevocably.

He left behind the world of commerce and engaged a completely different outlook, with far-sighted goals and values. One aspect of this new life was to make him a household name, with an international reputation - it was his involvement with the niche world of dowsing.

Hamish joined the British Society Dowsers in 1983, and rapidly became a stalwart member and regular lecturer. He strongly supported the organisation and was actively involved in its annual Conferences right up to 2009.

Originally inspired by the equally legendary Fountain Group founder, Colin Bloy, and by the clairvoyant and healer Michael Colmer, Hamish made a series of groundbreaking dowsing discoveries during the 1980s and 1990's, which are described in his collaborative works, *The Sun and the Serpent, The Dance of the Dragon* and *In Search of the Southern Serpent.* These books captured the imagination of a whole new generation of practitioners. In so doing, he played a significant role in bringing the arcane art out of its relative obscurity, and in presenting it to a wider, younger and more ambitious audience, hungry for both a practical and an intuitive understanding of the emerging field of Earth Energy.

Hamish realised the immense value in teaching others to dowse, both as a skill in its own right and as a means to exploring a portal on to a completely different way of looking at reality. He took great personal pleasure in organising dowsing courses, many of which were held at his Cornish home. He also produced a comprehensive beginners guide to the subject, in 2002, entitled *The Definitive Wee Book of Dowsing.*

While Hamish is renowned across the globe for researching and lecturing on dowsing-related topics, he will also be remembered for two other important strands of a multi-faceted life.

Resulting from his changed world-view, Hamish engendered the formation, in 2006, of the Parallel Community - an organisation dedicated to linking together diverse groups in a number of countries that are seeking to build a more caring and a more positive future for mankind. With over 1,000 members around the globe, Hamish regarded the establishment of this group as a significant step in translating his own practical experience of the world beyond the five gross senses into action in the here and now.

His other claim to fame was in realising his boyhood dream of becoming a blacksmith. He made both functional and sculptural ironwork to an exceptional standard, one example of which was presented to the Russian Orthodox Cathedral in Kiev. He also established a one-man production line of hand-forged dowsing rods that will be greatly treasured by many of us.

Hamish wrote a premature autobiography, *It's Not Too Late,* in the 1990's, but many of his more important revelations were yet to come. A second volume, *A Life Divined,* describing his life and his discoveries, largely in his own words, is due to be published later in 2010.

He was both a genial and generous figurehead and an incandescent inspiration for international communities of dowsers and activists - and while several well-known dowsers have passed over in recent times, he will leave a rather larger gap in the pantheon than most.

Hamish Miller had a head start on most of the rest of us in understanding the world beyond the five senses, in that he had not one, but three out-of-body experiences on which to draw. He was quite convinced that he knew what would happen after his eventual demise - because he had already been there! In his own words he found the prospect of passing over as 'rather exciting', and that he was 'quite looking forward to it'. With that sort of attitude, it is perhaps not too surprising that he didn't seek to put off the end of this cycle indefinitely.

His final moments came, as he would have wished, at home in his adopted and beloved Cornwall, following a gentle and joyful Burns night with his wife, and fellow dowser, Ba. Many of us would have wished him to have delayed his next journey a little longer, but in hindsight we were very privileged to have enjoyed his presence for so long.

Nigel Twinn

Index